1922

SCENES FROM A TURBULENT YEAR

NICK RENNISON

Oldcastle Books

First published in 2021
by Oldcastle Books Ltd,
Harpenden, UK

oldcastlebooks.co.uk
@oldcastlebooks

A CIP catalogue record for this book is available from the British Library.

ISBN
978-0-85730-467-4 (Hardcover)
978-0-85730-468-1 (Ebook)

2 4 6 8 10 9 7 5 3 1

Typeset in 11.75 on 15.25pt Goudy Old Style
by Avocet Typeset, Bideford, Devon, EX39 2BP
Printed and bound in Great Britain by Clays Ltd, Elcograf S.p.A.

'The world broke in two in 1922 or thereabouts'
Willa Cather

Contents

1922

SCENES FROM A TURBULENT YEAR

Introduction

It was a decade with a distinctive character. Even at the time, those who were living through them recognised that the 1920s were unusual. They deserved a special status. In America, they were dubbed 'The Roaring Twenties' or 'The Jazz Age'; in France, they were 'Les Années Folles' ('The Crazy Years'). The world had just emerged from a war that had killed millions of people and a global pandemic that had ended the lives of tens of millions more. The so-called 'Spanish' flu, named because Spain had initially seemed one of the most severely hit countries, had first shown itself during the last months of the First World War. It had spread over the next few years, infections coming in several waves, until almost a third of the world's population is now estimated to have caught it and between 20 and 50 million people had died of it. (Some estimates put the number of fatalities even higher.) Those who had come of age during these years and survived the twin traumas of war and disease were often disoriented and directionless. They were, in the phrase coined by the expatriate American writer Gertrude Stein, the 'Lost Generation'. The only aim many of the members of this generation in Europe and America had was to enjoy themselves. In an era of dance crazes, Hollywood excess, illicit drinking and a relaxation of sexual morals, hedonism was the name of the game.

This determination to party was only one aspect of the 1920s. It was also a period of upheaval and change. Of all the years in this dramatic decade, 1922 was the most turbulent. It was a year which altered the map of the world. In the wake of the war, an empire tottered and fell. The Ottoman Empire, which had survived for 600 years, ended with its last sultan forced into exile. Even the British Empire, which reached its greatest extent in the 1920s, was showing signs of decay. In Ireland, the Anglo-Irish War had come to an end in late 1921. A peace treaty had been signed that created the Irish Free State but triggered a brutal civil war the following year. Egypt had been granted a diluted form of self-government. The independence movement in India was gaining strength. Elsewhere, new nations came into existence and older nations made radical changes in their politics. The last few days of 1922 saw the official foundation of the USSR, the Union of Soviet Socialist Republics. Earlier in the year, Mussolini and his Blackshirts had embarked on their 'March to Rome' which had resulted in Italy becoming the first fascist state.

In the arts, traditional forms were proving inadequate and writers, musicians and painters were seeking different means of expressing themselves. In Anglophone literature, the publication in February 1922 of arguably the most influential novel of the century (James Joyce's *Ulysses*) was followed in October by that of the most influential poem (TS Eliot's *The Waste Land*). In society, already changed by the trauma of war, the conventions and morals of the past seemed increasingly outmoded; new ways of thinking and behaving were making their appearance. My book aims to provide a portrait of this rollercoaster of a year.

INTRODUCTION

Through a series of snapshots of events, from murders to football matches, from epoch-changing events like the establishment of the Soviet Union to artistic landmarks, I have attempted to give some sense of what the world was like 100 years ago. Some of what follows will provide reminders that, in LP Hartley's famous words, 'the past is a foreign country; they do things differently there'; some passages will seem all too familiar.

A century later the influence of events from 1922 lives on in many different ways. Modern Ireland has been shaped by what happened in the country that year. The treatment of diabetes with insulin (see January) continues to save and improve lives. The little-known animator who established Laugh-O-gram Films in Kansas City (see May) went on to create a media empire that still plays a central role in popular culture today. Sport still holds the mass appeal it was just beginning to achieve in 1922. Racial divisions still plague modern societies. As we emerge from a worldwide pandemic not so dissimilar to the one experienced by an earlier generation, it's easy to understand the determination of so many people in 1922 just to enjoy themselves. I hope that all of these snapshots of a past that sometimes carries surprising echoes of the present prove entertaining and enlightening.

January

Soon after the year opens, one of the greatest scandals in Hollywood history is reignited by the second trial of 'Fatty' Arbuckle. New hope is brought to diabetes sufferers around the world by the first successful treatment of the disease with insulin. The death of Ernest Shackleton on an island in the South Atlantic brings the heroic era of polar exploration to a close. In London, the first performance of an unusual work combining poetry and music heralds the arrival of a major talent. In Washington DC, atrocious weather leads to disaster.

The 'Fatty' Arbuckle Scandal

On January 11, the second trial of the comedian and film star Roscoe 'Fatty' Arbuckle began. The spotlight of national media publicity was again about to fall on the American film industry and the place that was already synonymous with it. Little more than a decade earlier, Hollywood had been nothing but a small rural community a few miles northwest of Los Angeles, locally renowned for its citrus groves and vineyards. Then the film-makers arrived, in flight from restrictions to their activities on the East Coast and in search of the sun. By 1922, Hollywood was the capital of the booming American film industry. Amongst the movies released that year were *Blood and Sand*, featuring the screen's Latin lover Rudolph Valentino; *Foolish Wives*, directed by and starring the self-proclaimed genius Erich von Stroheim; and *Manslaughter*, one of Cecil B DeMille's earliest and most lurid melodramas, complete with an eye-catching 'orgy' scene. In June, Robert Flaherty's *Nanook of the North*, the story of an Inuit hunter and his family, opened in New York. Despite the scepticism of the many movie distributors who had turned it down on the grounds that nobody would be interested in the lives of 'Eskimos', it became the first commercially successful feature-length documentary in cinema history. It spawned a brief enthusiasm for all things 'Eskimo', including a Broadway song with the unforgettable lyrics, 'Ever-loving Nanook/Though you don't read a book/But, oh, how you can love!'

Throughout 1922, the comedians who had already become some of Hollywood's biggest stars, continued to make movies. Charlie Chaplin was the world's most famous man, his 'Little Tramp' persona familiar to audiences from Los Angeles to London to Soviet Russia. Chaplin himself had grown tired of the character's limitations and was eager to make longer movies. His first feature, *The Kid*, had been released the previous year; *Pay Day*, his last short, two-reeler, appeared in 1922. Chaplin's rival, Buster Keaton, had already appeared in his first feature-length movie, *The Saphead* from 1920, although all his releases in 1922 were short comedies. (Keaton was a friend of Arbuckle and had made his film debut, five years earlier, in a comedy starring the fat man.) Bespectacled Harold Lloyd, famous for undertaking his own, often dangerous stunts (the most memorable, which involved him hanging from the hands of a clock outside the top storey of a skyscraper, was from *Safety Last*, released the following year), was also making feature-length films. At the same time, other now half-forgotten comedians (Ben Turpin, Charley Chase, Snub Pollard) were delighting audiences with their inventive, slapstick humour. A young English comic named Stan Laurel, who had been Chaplin's understudy in a music-hall troupe known as Fred Karno's Army, was starring as 'Rhubarb Vaselino' in *Mud and Sand*, a two-reel parody of *Blood and Sand*, and awaiting his meeting with destiny and a plump American actor named Oliver Hardy. (Laurel and Hardy actually appeared together in a 1921 short entitled *The Lucky Dog* but not as a double act.)

However, the year's blockbuster (although the word had yet to be invented) was *Robin Hood*, directed by Allan Dwan and starring Douglas Fairbanks Sr., 'King of Hollywood' during the silent era. Fairbanks was then at the height of his success and had demonstrated his talent for athletic swashbuckling in earlier films such as *The Mark of Zorro* and *The Three Musketeers*. On the lookout for another historical costume role, Fairbanks was initially dismissive of the suggestion of Robin Hood. He didn't want, he said, to play 'a flat-footed Englishman walking through the woods' but he was soon persuaded that the part could be tailored for his particular brand of energetic heroism. By the beginning of 1922, he was the project's most eloquent advocate. Vast sums were spent on creating a huge castle set and a reconstruction of twelfth-century Nottingham in the Pickford-Fairbanks Studio on the corner of Santa Monica Boulevard and Formosa Avenue in Hollywood. When *Robin Hood* premiered at the recently built Grauman's Egyptian Theatre on Hollywood Boulevard in October 1922, it had become the costliest movie in the history of cinema. More than $1,400,000 had been lavished on it.

And then, in this same year of 1922, there were the second and third trials of Fatty Arbuckle. What was to become one of the greatest scandals in Hollywood's history had begun at a party the previous year. The party was not in Hollywood. It was not even in Los Angeles. Many of the burgeoning film industry's glitterati had taken to driving along the coast to San Francisco to seek more discreet and anonymous surroundings in which to have a good time than they could find in Hollywood. On Labor Day weekend in September 1921, Roscoe 'Fatty' Arbuckle and two friends arrived at the St Francis Hotel in San Francisco where they had rooms and a suite booked. The bootleg liquor was soon flowing (this was the Prohibition era) and more guests began to show up. Among them were two young women – Maude Delmont and Virginia Rappe. Rappe was attractive, twenty-six years old and had worked as both a model and an actress in minor movie roles. Delmont was a more enigmatic figure with a dubious reputation. It later emerged that she had a track record as a procurer of women for wealthy men and as a blackmailer.

There were conflicting accounts of what happened next at the ongoing carousal in the St Francis Hotel. What is clear is that, as more and more booze was consumed, Virginia Rappe became distressed and ill. The hotel doctor was called but, after examining her, decided that she was suffering from no more than severe intoxication. She was left to sleep off the effects of the hooch in another room. The doctor was badly mistaken. A couple of days later, by which time Arbuckle and his friends had left San Francisco, Rappe was admitted to hospital. She died there on 9 September from a ruptured bladder and ensuing peritonitis.

According to Delmont, her friend was the victim of a sexual assault by Arbuckle. He had pulled the drunken Rappe into a room with the words, 'I've waited for you five years, and now I've got you', and shut and locked the door. When Delmont, hammering and kicking furiously on the door after she heard screaming in the room, finally persuaded the comedian to open up, she could see Rappe stretched out on the bed, moaning and in pain. It was at that point that she was taken to another room and the hotel doctor summoned. After her hospitalisation, she had told Delmont that Arbuckle had raped her.

Arbuckle, denying any wrongdoing, told a very different story. Yes, he had drunk with Virginia Rappe but he had never been alone with her, and others could confirm this. She had, at one point, become hysterical and started tugging at her clothes, claiming she couldn't breathe. Later he had found her throwing up in the bathroom and, together with some of the other partygoers, had arranged for her to be transferred to another room in the hotel so she could sleep off her intoxication. When he returned to Los Angeles after the weekend party, he assumed that she would be suffering from nothing worse than a monumental hangover.

Whether or not Arbuckle was telling the truth, he was in deep trouble. Delmont's story, when it emerged after Virginia Rappe's death, was like red meat to the tabloid press. Roscoe 'Fatty' Arbuckle was one of Hollywood's best-known and best-loved stars. A former vaudeville performer who weighed in at more than 300 pounds (hence his all too predictable nickname), he had been appearing in films since 1909. His popularity was such that Paramount Pictures had offered him a three-year contract worth $3 million in 1918. Just before the scandal broke they had renewed it for another year and another million dollars. Accusations against a man so much in the public eye made for eye-catching headlines. William Randolph Hearst, the press tycoon, later reported that the Arbuckle scandal had sold more newspapers than any event since the sinking of the *Lusitania* in 1915.

With ever more lurid accusations of sexual depravity surfacing in the newspapers, Arbuckle came back to San Francisco and voluntarily turned himself in. He spent three weeks in jail, as a mugshot of him was released to the papers and the authorities decided what to do. The

San Francisco District Attorney, Matthew Brady, was an ambitious man who saw the case as a means of self-publicity. He pressed for prosecution, originally on a charge of first-degree murder. This was reduced to one of manslaughter and Arbuckle's first trial by jury rather than by media began on 14 November 1921. He was accused of causing Rappe's death by rupturing her bladder during a sexual assault. (Even more sensational rumours were circulating that her injuries had been inflicted when Arbuckle, rendered impotent by too much alcohol, had penetrated her with a Coke or champagne bottle.) Many of Brady's prosecution witnesses provided testimony that was either contradictory or persuasively rebutted by the defence. Arbuckle took the stand himself and gave a measured account of what he said had happened at the party, denying all responsibility for Rappe's death. He must have had high hopes that his ordeal would soon be over but the trial ended in deadlock with the jury divided 10-2 in favour of acquittal. A mistrial was declared.

A second trial, which began on 11 January 1922, again ended with the jury unable to make a unanimous decision. Much of the same evidence was presented as in the first trial but the defence now had further means to discredit prosecution witnesses. One woman admitted that she had lied; another, a security guard who worked at the film studio and had testified that Arbuckle had once offered him a bribe to gain access to Virginia Rappe's dressing room, turned out to be facing his own criminal charges of assaulting an eight-year-old girl. The defence team was so confident that they decided not to ask the comedian to enter the witness box and give evidence himself. This ploy probably backfired. Some members of the second jury may well have concluded that he had something to hide. This time the division was 9-3 but in favour of a guilty verdict. With a mistrial again declared, Arbuckle's ordeal continued and a third trial opened on 13 March.

By this time, stories of the infamous party at the St Francis Hotel and of Hollywood orgies in general had been titillating newspaper readers for months. Many film distributors and cinema owners, not bothering with tiresome details of Arbuckle's guilt or innocence, had already banned his films. Yet the comedian's defence team had even stronger material to present to the jury than in either of the other trials. Maud Delmont's blackmailing past was revealed; evidence was put forward that showed Virginia Rappe was not the near-saintly innocent the prosecution had depicted. At least one key prosecution witness had done a bunk. Arbuckle again testified himself and made a good impression. The jury took less than ten minutes to declare Arbuckle not guilty. More than that, they insisted on writing a formal statement in which they said, 'Acquittal is not enough for Roscoe Arbuckle. We feel that a great injustice has been done him.' After the verdict was announced, all twelve members of the jury queued up to shake the defendant by the hand.

However, the damage had already been done. Although he had endured three trials and been acquitted in the last of these, Arbuckle's career was effectively over. Loyal friends came to his aid. Buster Keaton hired him as a writer on some of his short comedies. Under the name William Goodrich (Keaton originally suggested the punning pseudonym of Will B Good), Arbuckle directed a handful of movies for smaller studios. Ironically, the film that was probably his highest-profile work after the trials, *The Red Mill*, starred Marion Davies, the long-term mistress of William Randolph Hearst, the man whose newspapers had done so much to bring him down. However, the smears and innuendo that had haunted him since Virginia Rappe's death were never forgotten. He was a broken man. The now cult actress Louise Brooks, who worked with him on a 1931 film, said of him, 'He just sat in his director's chair like a dead man. He had been very nice and sweetly dead ever since the scandal that ruined his career.' Roscoe 'Fatty' Arbuckle died in his sleep of a heart attack on 29 June 1933, aged 46.

The Arbuckle scandal was a tragedy for the individuals involved. A young woman died in terrible circumstances. A much-loved movie comedian saw his career go down the drain. It also had wider repercussions. After the shock of the William Desmond Taylor murder (see February) followed the yellow press revelations surrounding Virginia Rappe's death, the Hollywood studios began to realise that they needed to do something to protect the industry's rapidly deteriorating reputation. Leading producers came together to create the MPPDA (the Motion Picture Producers and Distributors of America) in order to do so. In 1922, William Hays, the fiercely moralistic, former campaign manager of the US president, Warren Harding, was appointed the MPPDA's first chairman. Hays, 'a man of exemplary dullness' as one writer has described him, was charged in effect with creating a self-censorship board for Hollywood films. Fearing that more central censorship might be imposed upon them (there were already plenty of individual state regulations), the producers and distributors wanted to show that they could put their own house in order. Over the years to come, the 'Hays Office', as it came to be known, issued guidelines on what was and was not acceptable on screen, particularly in the portrayal of sex and violence. They were not always followed but, in 1930, a formal 'Production Code' was established. Four years later, the Production Code Administration came into being to enforce the often rigid regulations. All movies had to gain the PCA's approval before they could be shown. The Code continued in existence until the 1960s by which time society and the movie industry had changed so much that it had become unenforceable.

Insulin Treats Diabetes

On 11 January, a 13-year-old schoolboy from Toronto named Leonard Thompson made medical history when he became the first patient suffering from diabetes to be injected with insulin. Weighing only 65 pounds and drifting in and out of a diabetic coma as he lay in his bed at Toronto General Hospital, Leonard was close to death when his father agreed that he should be given the insulin. It had never previously been tried on a human being. The first dose had no effect on the boy's condition. In fact, it induced an allergic reaction but he was injected with a purer version of the insulin 12 days later and this time it worked. His blood glucose levels returned to normal and his most dangerous symptoms began to disappear.

Insulin's therapeutic potential had been proposed by

the Canadian physician and scientist Frederick Banting, working in conjunction with a younger colleague Charles Best, and they had presented their ideas to JJR Macleod, professor of physiology at the University of Toronto, the previous year. Macleod had encouraged them, provided them with grants and laboratory space, and had made his own contributions to the experiments designed to produce insulin that could be used on diabetic patients. Macleod and Banting, who was still only in his early thirties, were awarded the Nobel Prize in Medicine in 1923. Leonard Thompson lived for another 13 years, dying of pneumonia, a complication of his diabetes, in April 1935, aged 26.

The Death of Shackleton

The first week of 1922 saw the death of Ernest Shackleton, a man hailed at the time as one of the British Empire's greatest heroes. Born in Ireland and educated at Dulwich College, London, he had served as an officer in the Merchant Navy before joining Captain Scott's *Discovery* expedition and embarking on the career that made him one of the most famous of all polar explorers. Invalided home after his exertions on a journey with Scott and Edward Wilson to what was then the furthest south men had ever reached, Shackleton had returned to lead his own expedition to Antarctica and made it to within 100 miles of the South Pole in January 1909 before being forced to turn back. He had led the Imperial Trans-Antarctic Expedition of 1914-17 during which he took part in an epic boat journey to South Georgia to seek help for his men stranded on an uninhabited island in the Southern Ocean. His last voyage had begun in a blaze of publicity when his ship, the *Quest*, a converted Norwegian sealer, sailed from London on 17 September 1921. The ship proved a problem from the start and Shackleton had to change his plans several times en route south to accommodate delays caused by the need to work on its engines. By the time the *Quest* reached Rio at the end of November, he was in poor spirits. His aims for the expedition seemed uncertain. 'The Boss says,' one man confided to his diary, 'quite frankly that he does not know what he will do.' The plan, such as it was, appeared to be to head for the Antarctic islands and review the possibilities there. The truth was that Shackleton was ill. He died of a heart attack in South Georgia, aged only 47, on 5 January 1922. Plans were made to return his body to Britain but a message was received from his wife, saying that he should be buried on South Georgia. His grave now stands in the cemetery at Grytviken where it is regularly visited by tourists on the cruise ships that now sail Antarctic waters.

With Shackleton's passing what has often been termed 'The Heroic Age of Polar Exploration' came to an end. Of the other great figures of that era, Captain Scott was, of course, ten years dead, the failure of his attempt to be first to the South Pole already transformed into the stuff of legends, not least by Scott himself in the final journal entries he wrote as the end approached. In 1922, Apsley Cherry-Garrard, who had been one of the party which discovered the bodies of Scott and his companions, provided a less self-mythologising account when he published *The Worst Journey in the World*. Cherry-Garrard was frank about the dangers and discomforts he endured.

'Polar exploration,' he wrote, 'is at once the cleanest and most isolated way of having a bad time which has been devised.' (The 'worst journey' of his title does not refer to the doomed race to the pole but to an earlier trip on which Cherry-Garrard accompanied Edward Wilson and 'Birdie' Bowers, travelling from the expedition's base at Cape Evans to Cape Crozier. The journey was made in the midst of an Antarctic winter, in complete darkness and in temperatures that fell to more than 70° below zero. Its aim was to gather penguin eggs.) Cherry-Garrard's record of Scott's last expedition has become a classic of travel literature and remains in print a century after its first publication.

Roald Amundsen, the Norwegian who had beaten Scott to the South Pole, was still seeking glory. In 1922, he abandoned plans for a naval expedition to the North Pole and turned his attention to the idea of an aerial trip to the top of the world. Although other triumphs awaited him (he made a successful flight over the North Pole before his disappearance in 1928 during a search for the missing airship *Italia*), the nature of heroism was changing in the 1920s. After the horrors of the First World War, old ideals of manly endeavour often seemed hollow and inappropriate to many people.

First Performance of Façade

The fledgling composer William Walton had been 'discovered' at Oxford, where he was a choral scholar, by Sacheverell Sitwell, youngest member of a trio of literary siblings. Convinced of his musical genius, Sacheverell, in alliance with his brother Osbert and his sister Edith, had adopted the young man and, as 1922 began, he was living in an attic room at the family home, 2, Carlyle Square, London, dependent financially on their support. 'I went for a few weeks,' he later wrote, 'and stayed for fifteen years.' It was while he was there that he wrote musical accompaniment to a series of poems by Edith. Dubbed an 'entertainment', *Façade* has become a landmark in the history of twentieth-century English music. Walton continued to revise and add to the music for much of the rest of his life.

Façade's first private performance was given to invited guests at Carlyle Square on 24 January. Edith Sitwell recited her own idiosyncratic poems, declaiming 18 of them through a type of megaphone known as a Sengerphone which looks, in photographs, like a traffic cone upended so that someone can shout through the narrower end. It was invented by a Swiss singer named Alexander Senger, supposedly to give added volume to Wagnerian performers. Walton himself, still only a teenager, conducted the small ensemble of musicians.

In an expanded version, the first public performance took place in June the following year at the Aeolian Hall in New Bond Street. It was attended, according to one dismissive newspaper report, by 'the long-haired men and short-haired women' of London's avant-garde. Other newspapers were even ruder. One headline supposedly read, 'Drivel That They Paid to Hear'. Even some of the musicians didn't enjoy playing the score. The clarinettist is reported to have asked the composer, 'Mr Walton, has a clarinet player ever done you an injury?' However, it was the *succès de scandale* which the Sitwells had sought and propelled both them and Walton into the public eye.

The Knickerbocker Storm

For two days and nights in January a blizzard battered Washington DC. It was the city's worst snowstorm of the twentieth century. It began during the late afternoon of 27 January and within 24 hours most of Washington was lying under several feet of snow. More was to accumulate the next night. The 'Knickerbocker Storm', as it came to be known, took its name from the Knickerbocker Theatre, a movie palace in the city which was the site of the greatest loss of life during the atrocious weather. On the night of 28 January, the theatre was showing *Get-Rich-Quick Wallingford*, a silent film version of a bestselling novel of the day. The audience sat happily through a number of shorts and cartoons but, shortly after the feature film began, at around 9 pm, some of its members heard what they later described as a hissing noise from above. The Knickerbocker's flat roof was piled high with snow and it was starting to crack under the weight. Lumps of plaster from the ceiling began to fall on the cinemagoers. Many of them, realising the danger, ran for the exits or tried to shelter beneath the seats. It was too late. Within minutes the entire roof, detached from the supporting walls, fell. In doing so, it also pulled down the theatre's balcony and people who had so recently been looking forward to *Get-Rich-Quick Wallingford* were buried beneath the debris.

An operator at the local telephone company received a desperate call just after 9 pm: 'The roof of the Knickerbocker Theatre has just caved in. Send the nearest doctor.' She was later congratulated for the speed and quick-thinking with which she responded but rescue efforts were initially hampered by the difficulties in getting ambulances and other emergency vehicles to the scene because of the appalling weather conditions. By midnight, however, more than 200 police, soldiers and firemen were digging through the wreckage of the theatre in search of survivors. Two hours later, the numbers of would-be rescuers had tripled and efforts to free those trapped went on well into the next day. Many people were plucked from the debris alive but there were dozens of deaths. Every hospital in the area was overwhelmed by casualties and makeshift first-aid stations were set up in nearby businesses, including one in a sweet shop. A temporary morgue was established in the basement of a Christian Science church. It was soon besieged by people seeking news of missing loved ones. According to the *Washington Post*, there were 'pathetic scenes as men and women identified their sons, daughters, mothers, wives, and sweethearts among the dead'.

Stories soon emerged of terrible deaths and near-miraculous escapes. Survivor Mary Forsyth spent time pinned beneath the wreckage. Next to her, also trapped were a young man and his date. Amidst the cries of pain, Mary later recalled, the young man began to sing and his girlfriend's voice joined his. They both continued to sing for some time until their voices faded and they passed out. Their bodies were unearthed from the rubble the following day. Agnes Mellon attended the theatre with her boyfriend. When the roof fell, the crash was accompanied by a sudden outrush of air. Agnes's date was blown out into the lobby and survived; Agnes herself was struck by falling concrete and died. Rescuers in the early hours of the morning, digging through the wreckage, came across a large air pocket in which a man was still sitting bolt upright in his theatre seat. The man was dead. He had survived the initial collapse of the building but the shock had caused him to suffer a fatal heart attack. The final death toll of the Knickerbocker Storm was 98 and more than 130 were injured. It remains one of the worst disasters in the history of the USA's capital city.

February

One of the most significant works of twentieth-
century literature is published in Paris on its author's
40th birthday. In Rome, Catholics hail the election
of a new pope. The modern 'Bluebeard' goes to the
guillotine in France. Airships look like the future of
international travel but a crash in Norfolk, Virginia
sounds a warning. The mysterious murder of a well-
known director causes further scandal in Hollywood. A
demonstration in a small town in India leads to tragedy.
In Finland, the newly independent country is shocked
by a political assassination. Egypt is granted nominal
independence by Britain.

Joyce and Ulysses

The Irish novelist James Joyce was a man superstitiously obsessed with the significance of dates. Famously, the events of *Ulysses*, his most widely known work and, some would argue, the most significant novel of the twentieth century, unfold on 16 June 1904, the day he went on his first date with Nora Barnacle, the woman who was to become his partner for life. He was determined that *Ulysses* should be published on 2 February 1922. Not only was this his 40th birthday but Joyce also liked the numerological coincidence of 2/2/22.

Getting the manuscript ready for that auspicious date was no easy task. As those who have read *Ulysses* will know, it was a manuscript likely to induce panic in any typist commissioned to make sense of it. Not only were Joyce's prose and style unusual, his handwriting was often indecipherable and the pages he produced were peppered with crossings-out and with arrows to indicate where he wanted the additional material scribbled in the margins to go. One typist had threatened suicide if forced to continue with the task; another had rung the bell of Joyce's apartment one morning, dumped the manuscript on the doorstep and run away.

The book was finally published, in an edition of 1,000 copies, by Sylvia Beach, the American expatriate owner of the Paris bookshop, Shakespeare and Company. (Substantial excerpts had previously been serialised in the magazine *The Little Review* between March 1918 and December 1920.) A further edition, of 2,000 copies, appeared later in the year, this time under the imprint of Egoist Press, established by Joyce's patron and admirer Harriet Shaw Weaver.

Joyce was able to celebrate both his 40th birthday and the publication of his masterpiece by dining at Ferrari's, one of his favourite Parisian restaurants, with his family and a select group of friends. At that time, there were only two copies of *Ulysses* in the French capital. (The other 998 were still with the printer in Dijon.) One was placed in the window of Shakespeare and Company; the other accompanied its author to Ferrari's. According to his biographer, Richard Ellmann, Joyce 'placed it under his chair... Everyone asked to see it opened, but he seemed to shrink from producing it. After the dessert, he at last untied the parcel and laid the book on the table.' A toast was proposed and Joyce, who had earlier looked surprisingly glum, now seemed moved by the occasion.

When copies reached the press later in the year, many of the reviews were unsurprisingly bad. Neither Joyce nor anyone else would have expected the reviewer at the *Daily Express* to like the book and SPB Mais did not disappoint. 'Our first impression is that of sheer disgust,' he began and concluded that, 'Reading Mr Joyce is like making an excursion into Bolshevist Russia: all standards go by the board.' For some unfathomable reason, the *Sporting Times*, much better known for its coverage of horse-racing than for its interest in modern literature, also chose to review Joyce's masterpiece. It's fair to say that its writer didn't like it. 'The main contents are enough to make a Hottentot sick,' he opined and went on to tell his readers that it 'appears to have been written by a perverted lunatic who has made a specialty of the literature of the latrine.'

The poet Alfred Noyes, now remembered, if at all, for 'The Highwayman', his jaunty ballad about a gentleman of the road and his ill-fated love affair, was nearly apoplectic with horror after looking at it. 'It is simply the foulest book that has ever found its way into print,' he reported.

Even some of those readers who might have been expected to appreciate what Joyce was attempting were dismissive. Virginia Woolf was herself a leading light of modernism but her opinions of *Ulysses* often seem motivated more by social snobbery than literary insight. 'An illiterate, underbred book it seems to me,' she confided to her diary in August, 'the book of a self-taught working man, & we all know how distressing they are, how egotistic, insistent, raw, striking and ultimately nauseating.' She also described it as 'the work of a queasy undergraduate scratching his pimples.'

There were, of course, readers who understood and appreciated Joyce's genius. The American Gilbert Seldes, a literary critic and a pioneer in the academic appreciation of popular culture, wrote that, 'this epic of defeat, in which there is not a scamped page nor a moment of weakness, in which whole chapters are monuments to the power and glory of the written word, is itself a victory of the creative intelligence over the chaos of uncreated things.'

For many years, that perhaps mythical beast, the 'common reader', would find it difficult to express an opinion on *Ulysses* one way or another. Because of its alleged obscenity, it was banned from being published in Britain, the United States and many other countries. Joyce's novel became literary contraband, only to be read if you could get your hands on a pirated edition or had access to one which had been smuggled through customs.

A New Pope

For tens of millions of Catholics, the early months of the year brought the death of one pope and the election of another. Benedict XV had been raised to the papacy in the very month that the First World War broke out and his pontificate had been shaped by the conflict, which he once described as 'the suicide of civilised Europe', and by its aftermath. One of his primary concerns in his last year in office was the growing persecution of Catholics around the world, particularly in Soviet Russia. At the beginning of January 1922, Benedict fell ill with pneumonia. His condition worsened rapidly and he died on the 22nd of that month. The Papal Conclave to elect his successor began on 2 February. It did not prove an easy decision. The cardinals divided into two camps, a conservative faction led by the Spaniard Rafael Merry del Val and a more liberal grouping supporting Pietro Gasparri, an Italian who had been Cardinal Secretary of State under Benedict. Over the course of thirteen ballots and four days, no candidate could gain the two-thirds majority that was required for election. Achille Ratti, Archbishop of Milan, was proposed as a compromise candidate, although he was reluctant to put himself forward. He had only been made a cardinal the previous year. However, on the fifth day and fourteenth ballot, he received 38 votes, enough to place him on the papal throne. When a small delegation approached him to ask if he was willing to accept the responsibility, he continued to sound unenthusiastic about the prospect. 'As it is God's will, it cannot be refused,' was the most he would say. 'Since it is the will of God I must obey.' It was enough.

The white smoke issued from the chimney on the roof of the Sistine Chapel to indicate that a decision had been reached and Ratti was elected, taking the name Pius XI.

Henri Landru Executed

High-profile murder cases across the world hit the headlines during 1922. February saw the conclusion to events which had been front page news in France for a long time. Henri Landru was executed outside the gates of a prison in Versailles. Nicknamed the 'Bluebeard of Gambais' (the village where he lived), Landru had killed at least seven women between 1915 and 1919, most of whom he had met through lonely hearts advertisements he had placed in newspapers. Pushed into action by the half-sister of one of his victims, who began her own investigations, the police had eventually arrested Landru in April 1919. The case against him was built up over the next two years and his trial, in November 1921, had resulted in conviction and the presiding judge sentencing him to the guillotine.

The American journalist Webb Miller witnessed the public execution on 25 February. 'The slayer was conducted a short distance from the gates to the guillotine, which had been erected in the middle of a street, running past the prison,' Miller wrote. 'He was pushed against an upright board and hastily tied. The board fell forward and was shoved underneath the machine. The executioner jerked a cord, the knife with its heavy weights flickered down with a thud, Landru's head toppled off into a basket and the execution was over – all in the space of a few seconds.'

Landru's death did not end fascination with his crimes. Over the century since he met his end, his story has been rehashed and retold in novels, plays and films. Chaplin's 1947 black comedy *Monsieur Verdoux* is loosely based on it. Claude Chabrol's *Landru* from 1963 is an imaginative retelling of the murderer's career. On its release, a woman named Fernande Segret sued Chabrol for defamation. She was Landru's last mistress and was distressed by the way she had been portrayed in the movie.

The Roma Crashes

At the beginning of the 1920s, airships were seen by many as the future of travel. Zeppelins, first patented by their inventor, Graf Ferdinand von Zeppelin in the 1890s, had shown their military worth in the First World War but once peace had come, there were soon plans to use airships to transport paying passengers rather than bombs. In 1922, the British company, Vickers Ltd, came up with the 'Burney Scheme', named after its major proponent, Sir Dennistoun Burney, to build six airships, at a cost of £4 million. These would provide a passenger service which would link British colonies and dominions around the world. In the coming years, this was to evolve into the

Imperial Airships Scheme, supported by government throughout the decade and into the 1930s.

There were, however, already alarming indications that airships might not be the safest way to take to the skies. The *Roma* was built by the Italian company in which the famous aviator and polar explorer Umberto Nobile was one of the partners. After making successful trial flights in 1920, it was sold to the US Army the following year. Entirely dismantled, it was shipped from Italy to America in bits and there reassembled. Further test flights followed but disaster struck in Norfolk, Virginia in February 1922. The airship's rudder system failed. What happened next was described by a newspaper report at the time. 'As the big dirigible plunged to earth, it capsized across a high-tension electric line, bursting in a roaring furnace of blazing hydrogen gas... Many hours after her fall, the ship was still a mass of flames from end to end of her 140-foot mass. The fire fed on the million cubic feet of gas which had distended the great bag for flight and made all attempt at rescue futile.' A small number of those aboard survived, with serious injuries, by jumping from the airship just before it struck the ground. Most of the crew of the *Roma* were trapped inside and stood no chance. Its captain, an experienced aviator named Dale Mabry, and 33 others died in the flames.

In retrospect, the crash of the *Roma* can be seen as the beginning of the end of the dream of giant airships circling the world in a new era of exciting, glamorous travel. Plans, including the Imperial Airways Scheme, were pursued but further, more highly publicised crashes followed. The British airship, the *R101*, crashed in France on its maiden overseas flight in 1930, killing 48 of the 54 people on board, including Lord Thomson, air minister at the time. The Labour government abandoned the development of airships the following year. In 1937, the German airship, the *Hindenburg*, caught fire as it tried to dock at an air station in New Jersey. Thirteen passengers and twenty-two crew died in the ensuing blaze. Public confidence in the safety of airships was badly dented. The era of the giant dirigibles was over.

Who Killed Bill Taylor?

Across the rest of America, and around the world, Hollywood in the early 1920s was not only gaining a reputation for extravagance in pursuit of entertainment, it was also becoming a byword for sin and decadence. For many ordinary Americans it was already a factory of dreams; for others it was a modern Babylon located in the heart of California. Events of 1922 did nothing to dispel the image. Instead they magnified it. Hollywood was increasingly seen as a hotbed of drink, drugs and illicit sex. To a large extent, it was exactly that. Despite Prohibition, alcohol flowed freely in the movie capital. Unsurprisingly, many of the beautiful young men and women who appeared on the screen were jumping into bed with one another. And drugs of all kinds were readily available. Some careers and lives were wrecked by them. Wallace Reid had had significant roles in DW Griffith's pioneering epics *The Birth of a Nation* and *Intolerance*, and had gone on to become one of Hollywood's sexiest leading men, described as 'the screen's most perfect lover' by a much-read movie magazine. By 1922, he was hopelessly dependent on morphine, his addiction allegedly fostered and made worse by studio bosses who encouraged his drug use to keep him working. He died in a rehabilitation clinic in January 1923, aged 31.

Drugs, booze and promiscuity could often be kept secret. Murder was another matter. The killing of a prominent Hollywood director could not be kept out of the newspapers. William Desmond Taylor was a public-school-educated product of the Anglo-Irish gentry who had travelled to America as a young man. He entered the film industry as an actor but rapidly became one of the industry's most reliably effective directors, working on more than 50 films. Early on the morning of 2 February 1922, his body was found lying on the floor of the living room in his Los Angeles bungalow. A man claiming to be a doctor examined it and said he had died of a stomach haemorrhage. The 'doctor' then faded into the crowd of onlookers who had gathered and was never seen again. His medical credentials were immediately brought into question when Taylor's body was rolled over and it became clear that the director had actually been shot in the back some hours earlier. He had been murdered.

Although Taylor was reported to have been a popular figure in Hollywood, there was no shortage of candidates for his killer. His former valet Edward Sands, a man of many aliases and previous criminal convictions, was one suspect but he disappeared on the day of the murder and the police were never able to track him down. Sands's replacement as Taylor's manservant, a black man named

Henry Peavey, also aroused suspicion but the police soon decided he was not the murderer. (One imaginative woman reporter, convinced that Peavey was the killer and that he was terrified of ghosts, arranged for a confederate to impersonate Taylor, returned from the grave to confront Peavey. The idea was to scare him into a confession. Peavey laughed in the supposed spectre's face.)

Most titillating for newspaper readers across the country was the possible involvement of two female movie stars. Mabel Normand, who had co-starred with Chaplin in many of his early movies, was a close friend and the last person to see Desmond alive. She was interrogated by police who briefly considered her a suspect. They soon dismissed the idea but her career suffered. Her tangential involvement in another scandal two years later, when her chauffeur shot and wounded an oil millionaire, did not help. She made only a handful more films before her death in 1930, at the age of 37. A few days before she died, she is reputed to have asked a friend, 'Do you think they'll ever find out who killed Bill Taylor?'

Mary Miles Minter was a former child star who had appeared in a number of films which Desmond had directed. Love letters she had written to him were found in his home after his death but it is not clear whether the couple ever were lovers. There was a 30-year age gap between them and he may have seen himself more as a father figure to her than a lover. So may she. Minter's domineering mother, a Broadway actress named Charlotte Shelby, was also long considered a candidate for the role of Desmond's killer. She had promoted her daughter's career with steely-eyed determination and was overprotective of her long after she had ceased to be a child. She had reportedly threatened other men who had shown a more than fatherly interest in Mary. Indeed, she is said to have been heard yelling at Taylor, 'If I ever catch you hanging around Mary again, I'll blow your goddamned brains out!' Some writers on the case have claimed that the mysterious figure, a man with 'an effeminate walk', whom one witness saw outside the Taylor bungalow the previous evening was Shelby in male attire. Nothing has ever been proved. Indeed no theory about Taylor's death – and there have been plenty of them – has ever been conclusively shown to be anything other than that – a theory. It seems that the answer to Mabel Normand's question may well be, 'No – they never will.'

Chauri Chaura

On 4 February, demonstrators in the town of Chauri Chaura, in what is now the Indian state of Uttar Pradesh, clashed with police. In the early 1920s, Mahatma Gandhi's nationwide Non-Cooperation Movement, which used peaceful means to challenge the government and push towards ultimate independence, was gaining strength throughout the country. It spread even into small towns like Chauri Chaura where, at the beginning of the month, volunteers working for the movement, led by a retired soldier named Bhagwan Ahir, demonstrated against high food prices. The police responded by inflicting a beating on Ahir and several others. Unsurprisingly, this merely served to inflame an already volatile situation.

The following Saturday, 4 February, a crowd gathered to march to the local police station in protest. There were also plans to picket the bazaar. Forewarned of what was intended, the police chief in Chauri Chaura had asked for reinforcements from nearby townships.

The idea was to intimidate the crowd into abandoning plans to march on the bazaar. It failed to do so. Tempers grew increasingly frayed on both sides, stones were hurled at the police, and an officer gave the order to fire in the air. Some in the crowd, unaware that the shooting had been cautionary rather than targeted, thought the bullets had been made miraculously ineffective. A cry of 'Bullets have turned into water by the grace of Gandhiji' was heard as the warning shots were ignored, and the crowd only pressed closer to the now beleaguered policemen. Panicking, they directed live ammunition into the mass of protesters. Three people were killed and more wounded. Undeterred, the demonstrators continued to advance and the policemen, greatly outnumbered, retreated to their station house. They were locked in and the crowd poured kerosene on to the police station's walls before setting it alight. Trapped in the flames, at least 22 of the policemen, including the station commander, died.

By nightfall on 4 February the crowd had dispersed but both the authorities and the nationalists reacted quickly. Homes were raided and arrests made. Devdas Gandhi, the nationalist leader's son, arrived in the area and established a Chauri Chaura Support Fund to offer monetary assistance to those on both sides in the confrontation and 'to atone for this sudden and inauspicious mishap'. Gandhi himself, the inspiration behind the Non-Cooperation Movement and a profound believer in the need for peaceful protest only, was appalled by what had happened. He felt partially responsible and embarked on a five-day fast as a penance. He also proposed a general suspension of mass civil disobedience and, a week after the events at Chauri Chaura, this was enacted throughout India.

A Finnish Assassination

On 14 February, the Finnish Minister of the Interior, Heikki Ritavuori, was shot dead outside his home in Helsinki. In the years immediately after the First World War, Finland had emerged from a long period as part of the Russian Empire. After a short civil war and an equally brief experiment with monarchy, it was now an independent republic. Resentments and divisions from the war in 1918 between right- and left-wing factions still persisted in the early 1920s. Ritavuori, who had changed his original name of Rydman in 1906 to one that emphasised his Finnishness and his commitment to the cause of Finnish independence, was a liberal MP. He was a close associate of the new republic's first president, Kaarlo Ståhlberg, and became a favourite target for right-wing propagandists who disliked the policies of both men. One of the witnesses to the killing was Gerda Ryti, the wife of a future Finnish president, who said that she had seen a 'fat man' fire three shots at the minister.

The fat man turned out to be 45-year-old Knut Ernst Tandefelt, the scion of a Swedish-speaking aristocratic family. Tandefelt's mental health had been severely damaged by his experiences in a Russian prison during the First World War. Subjected to torture, he had been released a broken man but seemed to have had some success in putting his life back in order. Now he was persuaded by the right-wing press attacks that Ritavuori was a danger to the country. He decided the politician had to die. At 5 pm on 14 February, he followed Ritavuori as he walked to his house and pulled the gun from his pocket when the minister reached for the door handle. The pistol became entangled in Tandefelt's coat and he was close to (literally) shooting himself in the foot but he managed to tug it free and fire three shots at his target, hitting Ritavuori in the heart and lungs. Chased from the murder scene, he soon surrendered and made no attempt to deny his actions. Although there were strong suspicions that the assassin might have been manipulated by others who wanted Ritavuori out of the way, Tandefelt claimed at his trial that he had acted alone. A medical examination cast doubt on his sanity but he was nonetheless sentenced to 12 years of hard labour. He died in a mental asylum in 1948.

Egyptian Independence

Although the late Victorian period is usually seen as the heyday of the British Empire, in reality it reached its greatest size in 1919. With its acquisition of German colonies after the First World War, it became the empire on which, in line with the cliché, the sun literally never set. There was no point during the day when the sun was not shining somewhere in Britain's territories. Yet the largest empire the world had known began to shrink almost immediately. Our year of 1922 saw the beginnings of that reduction in Egypt.

The British had established a protectorate over Egypt after their victory in the Anglo-Egyptian War of 1882. Although the country was not formally part of the British Empire, it was, in effect, under British rule, and the most powerful man in the country for more than 20 years was Evelyn Baring, Earl of Cromer who was the British Consul-General in Egypt. In the aftermath of the First World War, and with Cromer long gone (he resigned his position in 1907 and died ten years later), there were growing demands for Egyptian independence. These were spearheaded by the Wafd Party and its leader Saad Zaghloul. Mass demonstrations in 1919 turned to riots which were brutally suppressed and hundreds of protesters were killed. Efforts on both sides to resolve the situation came to nothing. Zaghloul was arrested and exiled, first to Malta and then to the Seychelles. Martial law, which had been intermittently imposed on the country since 1914, was reasserted at the end of 1921. However, with violence in Cairo and elsewhere growing once more, some kind of solution was necessary. Viscount Allenby, Special High Commissioner in Egypt, came up with a set of proposals to reach a compromise.

On 28 February 1922, the government in London accepted Allenby's proposals and Egypt was granted nominal independence. The British issued the Unilateral Declaration of Egyptian Independence in which it was stated that 'the British Protectorate over Egypt is terminated and Egypt is declared to be an independent sovereign state.' The following month, the Sultan became King Fuad I. Zaghloul and other nationalists were released from exile in the Seychelles and, by the following year, were back in Egypt. Zaghloul became the Egyptian Prime Minister in January 1924. In reality, however, the ultimate reins of power were still in the hands of the British who retained the ability to intervene in Egyptian affairs if they felt the interests of the Empire were under threat. They were most concerned about their continuing control of the Suez Canal, vital to imperial trade and communications, and any threat to this from rival powers. The Unilateral Declaration specifically reserved four areas in which the British could continue to do as they wished in Egypt: the security of the Empire's communications; the defence of Egypt against foreign aggression; the protection of foreign interests and the protection of minorities; and the Sudan which was under joint Anglo-Egyptian control.

March

The European film industry competes with Hollywood
for home audiences. In Weimar Germany two great
directors emerge and the first major vampire movie
is released. A legendary baseball player signs a new
contract for the New York Yankees. Following a period
of mass civil disobedience, Mahatma Gandhi is arrested
and charged with sedition. Two daring Portuguese pilots
climb aboard a seaplane and take off from the Tagus
River in Lisbon to fly to Brazil. At a remote farmhouse
in Bavaria a shocking series of murders is discovered.
In America, F Scott Fitzgerald publishes his second
novel and he and his wife Zelda become icons of the
Jazz Age, a phrase he himself popularises. In Berlin the
father of a future novelist is the accidental victim of an
assassination attempt.

European Cinema and the Vampire Movie

It was not just in Hollywood that movies were being made which increasingly confirmed the cinema's status as the most popular of twentieth-century arts. In Britain, a plump young man from Leytonstone, who had started in the film industry three years earlier, working as a title-card designer for Islington Studios in Hoxton, was about to launch his directorial career. His name was Alfred Hitchcock. Most Hitchcock biographers agree that the first film project in which, still in his early twenties, he took the director's chair was a 1922 picture entitled *Number 13*. The movie, initially backed by Gainsborough Pictures, had problems with its budget and was pulled from production when no more cash was forthcoming. The few scenes that Hitchcock managed to shoot have all been lost. It was, he later remarked, 'a somewhat chastening experience'. In the same year, he may also have contributed to another mostly lost movie entitled *Always Tell Your Wife*. The well-known actor-manager Seymour Hicks was to star in a series of two-reeler comedies of which this was to be the first one. All were to be directed by a man named Hugh Croise but Croise either fell ill or fell out with his star. The project was about to be cancelled when, in Hicks's words, 'a fat youth who was in charge of the property room at the studio volunteered to help me'. This was, of course, Hitchcock. He and Hicks co-directed the film but only a handful of scenes survive. It is unclear which, if any, of these were Hitchcock's work and nobody knows for sure if the finished movie was ever shown to a paying audience.

In France, directors such as Julien Duvivier and Jacques

Feyder, who were to go on to long and productive careers, were making some of their first films. Italy, which had been home to some of the most spectacular epics of the early silent era, had seen a decline in its film-making in the early 1920s but major co-productions with American studios, such as *Nero* from 1922, still made it to the screen. Scandinavia had its own thriving film industries with the Danish director Carl Theodor Dreyer and the Swedes Mauritz Stiller and Victor Sjöström making their mark. Outside Europe, studios opened in Japan where increasingly ambitious movies were produced and, in India, the first films from what would later be called Bollywood were hitting the screens.

However, it was in Germany that some of the most adventurous and innovative films of the time were produced. Two directors in particular exemplified the creativity of Weimar-era movies. Born in Vienna in 1890, Fritz Lang had fought in the First World War and had drifted into the burgeoning movie industry in its aftermath. Graduating swiftly from writer to director, he worked with his future wife, the screenwriter Thea von Harbou, to create films which blended popular genres with the Expressionist designs and themes emerging in works like *The Cabinet of Dr Caligari*. (Indeed, Lang was first choice to direct this groundbreaking movie but had to turn down the job because of other commitments.) His *Dr Mabuse, der Spieler* ('Dr Mabuse, the Gambler'), released in April and May 1922 with a screenplay by him and von Harbou, was a two-part, four-hour-long epic about a criminal genius, based on a novel by Norbert Jacques, a Luxembourgish author who wrote in German. Lang returned to the character several times in his later career and *Die 1000 Augen des Dr Mabuse* ('The Thousand Eyes of Dr Mabuse') in 1960 was the last film he directed. Lang continued to work in Germany throughout the Weimar years, directing such classics as *Metropolis* and *M*. He left the country soon after the Nazis came to power, heading first for Paris and then for Hollywood.

Two years older than Lang, FW Murnau (real name Friedrich Wilhelm Plumpe) was obsessed by films from his student days at the University of Berlin. He fought in the First World War, joining the Imperial German Flying Corps and carrying out missions over the trenches, before he was obliged to make an emergency landing in neutral Switzerland. There he was interned and spent the remainder of the war in a POW camp. With the fighting over, Murnau was determined to make movies. His debut, *Der Knabe in Blau* ('The Boy in Blue') was released in 1919 but only fragments of it survive. He then joined forces with the actor Conrad Veidt (soon to be a big star in Germany but best remembered by English-speaking audiences as the Nazi officer Major Strasser in the Hollywood classic, *Casablanca*) to produce several more films, most of them now lost. One of these lost movies is *Der Janus-Kopf* ('The Head of Janus'), a version of the Jekyll and Hyde story in which a then obscure Hungarian actor named Bela Lugosi had a small role.

4 March 1922 saw the release of what remains Murnau's best-known film – *Nosferatu* which was premiered that day in the Marmorsaal ('Marble Hall') of the Berlin Zoological Garden. Guests were asked to arrive for the showing in appropriately nineteenth-century costume. Subtitled 'Eine

Symphonie des Grauens' ('A Symphony of Horror'), this was also cinema's first major tale of vampirism. (The previous year, a movie entitled *Drakula halála*, or *Dracula's Death*, was made in Hungary but it was only an hour long, had limited distribution and is now assumed to be lost. It also took very little beyond the name 'Dracula' from Bram Stoker's 1897 novel.) Eighty years later, the American film critic Roger Ebert could still describe *Nosferatu* as 'the best of all vampire movies' and write that, 'Its eerie power only increases with age.' Murnau's film was very clearly based on the Stoker novel but, because of difficulties over the copyright, names had to be changed and the plot significantly altered. Count Dracula became Count Orlok, Jonathan Harker Thomas Hutter and, although Orlok's castle was still located in Transylvania, much of the rest of the action took place not in Whitby, as in the book, but in the fictional German town of Wisborg (actually Wismar). The extraordinary appearance of Max Schreck, the actor playing Orlok, with his cadaverous face, bald head, bat-like ears and elongated fingernails, only adds to the effect of a movie which retains its ability to send a collective shiver up an audience's spine a century after it was made. (By happy coincidence, 'Max Schreck' in German could be interpreted as meaning 'extreme fear'.) Even with the alterations, Bram Stoker's widow and the estate were not impressed. They sued in an attempt to prevent the distribution of the film and most prints of it were destroyed by court order. A handful, which had already been despatched worldwide, survived the flames and the movie's reputation grew as the decades passed.

Like Lang – indeed several years earlier than Lang –

Murnau himself left Germany for Hollywood. He arrived in California in 1926 and his first American movie, *Sunrise*, although not a commercial success, won the Academy Award for 'Best Unique and Artistic Picture' at the very first Oscars ceremony. (The curiously named award was only ever presented this one time.)

In 1931, seven days before the premiere of his last film, *Tabu* (subtitled 'A Story of the South Seas'), Murnau was killed in a car crash. Garcia Stevenson, the director's teenage Filipino servant, who was driving the car, emerged unscathed. Scandalous Hollywood rumour suggested that Stevenson had been distracted at the wheel because Murnau, who was gay, was performing fellatio on him at the time.

Babe Ruth Signs a New Contract

In 1922, American baseball was going through a golden age. Although the sport was still recovering from the shock of the 1919 game-fixing scandal in which eight members of the Chicago White Sox, including the legendary 'Shoeless' Joe Jackson, were accused of throwing that year's World Series, it was an era when giants walked the land. The names of many from the 1920s still resonate with fans today. Jackson and his teammates had fallen from grace, but there were plenty of heroes to admire. Ty Cobb, nicknamed the 'Georgia Peach', had been a star since his first appearance for the Detroit Tigers as a teenager in 1905. He was now at the veteran stage but still capable of winning games. Other big names included 'Gorgeous'

George Sisler, Rogers Hornsby and Pie Traynor. The greatest of them all, and probably still the most famous individual in baseball history, was Babe Ruth.

George Herman 'Babe' Ruth was born in Baltimore in 1895, the son of a saloon-keeper of German ancestry (as a child the future sports star spoke German at home), and made his debut in professional baseball as a teenager, playing for the then minor-league team, the Baltimore Orioles. When he joined the Boston Red Sox in 1914, he was admired mainly for his ability as a pitcher but it was not long before his astonishing power as a hitter emerged. In 1919, his last season before moving from Boston to join the New York Yankees, he hit 29 home runs and was hailed as the sport's newest star. In his first season with his new team, he hit a remarkable 54 home runs, 10 more than the previous record for a season, and the following year he topped that with 59. He had become a phenomenon.

On 6 March 1922, Ruth signed a new three-year contract with the Yankees, worth what was then the staggering sum of $52,000 a year. It was more than twice what had been paid to any other baseball player previously and Ruth's earnings now made up 40 per cent of the Yankees' payroll for its players. All this was despite the fact that he was, at the time, suspended from playing because, contrary to major-league rules, he had participated in exhibition matches in the autumn of the previous year. Ruth was unrepentant. All he had been doing, he said, had been giving baseball fans 'an opportunity to see the big players in action'. And, of course, earning himself an extra dollar or two.

Ruth was always a difficult man to manage. He was a gluttonous eater and drinker whose weight yo-yoed alarmingly during his career. He was also an enthusiastic womaniser. His temper, on and off the field, was unpredictable. During a game at the end of May 1922, he threw dirt at the umpire and, when a spectator began to heckle him from the stands, Ruth left the pitch and set off in pursuit of him. He was unrepentant after the game finished. 'They can boo and hoot me all they want,' he told a reporter. 'But when a fan calls insulting names from the grandstand and becomes abusive, I don't intend to stand for it. This fellow today, whoever he was, called me a low-down bum and other names that got me mad... I would go into the stands again if I had to.' Furthermore, he pointed out, 'I didn't throw any dust in the umpire's face. It didn't go into his face, only on his sleeve.'

Gandhi on Trial

Britain may have been willing to relinquish a little of its grasp on Egypt (see February) but an arrest and trial in March showed that its determination to resist calls for Indian independence had not slackened. The most persistent thorn in the Raj's side in the early 1920s was Mahatma Gandhi. Born in Gujarat, Gandhi had trained as a lawyer in London and spent many years in South Africa where he had campaigned for the civil rights of fellow Indians subjected to racial discrimination. Returning to India in 1915 at the age of 45, he had thrown himself into the struggle for independence, joining the Indian National Congress party and advocating peaceful resistance to British rule. In 1920, Gandhi launched the

Non-Cooperation Movement, in response to increasingly repressive legislation and to the infamous Jallianwala Bagh massacre of the previous year, in which troops of the British Indian Army under the command of Brigadier-General Reginald Dyer had opened fire on an unarmed crowd in Amritsar, killing more than 350 people. Practising the principles of *satyagraha*, the particularly Gandhian form of civil disobedience, the Non-Cooperation Movement went from strength to strength throughout India. The British authorities increasingly saw Gandhi as a threat to stable government.

On 10 March 1922, he was arrested and put on trial for sedition. His specific offence was the writing of three articles for his *Young India* journal and the charge was that he was 'attempting to excite disaffection towards His Majesty's Government established by law in British India'. He appeared before the court, dressed in the loincloth which had become his habitual attire and which is now inextricably associated with the image most people have of him. Sarojini Naidu, a poet, political activist and advocate of women's rights, who was in the courtroom that day, noted that everyone present rose to their feet 'in an act of spontaneous homage' when Gandhi entered. According to Naidu, he looked around the court and remarked, 'This is like a family gathering and not a law court.' Gandhi made no attempt to claim his innocence of the charges. 'I have no desire whatsoever,' he announced, 'to conceal from this court the fact that to preach disaffection from the existing system of government has become almost a passion for me.' He pleaded guilty but, in a moving statement, he explained his reasons for his actions and writings. 'I have no personal ill-will against any single administrator,' he said, 'much less can I have any disaffection towards the King's person. But I hold it to be a virtue to be disaffected towards a government which in its totality has done more harm to India than any previous system.'

In reply, the judge, Mr Justice Broomfield, describing Gandhi as 'in a different category from any person I have ever tried', was fulsome in his praise of the man he was about to sentence. 'It would be impossible,' he stated, 'to ignore the fact that, in the eyes of millions of your countrymen, you are a great patriot and a great leader. Even those who differ from you in politics look upon you as a man of high ideals and of noble and even saintly life.' Despite his admiration for Gandhi, Broomfield sentenced him to six years of imprisonment, although he added that if a higher authority later decided to reduce the sentence, 'no one would be better pleased than I.' As the limited number of friends and followers who had been allowed into the building surrounded him, some touching his hands and others falling at his feet, a smiling Gandhi was led out of the courtroom to begin his sentence at the Sabarmati Jail in Ahmedabad. Transferred later in the month to Yerwada Central Jail in Pune, he was to be released in February 1924, less than two years into his sentence, because of failing health.

Stars of the Future

On 15 March an event took place for the first time at the Ambassador Hotel in Los Angeles which was to become a regular part of the Hollywood year for more than a decade. The Western Association of Motion Picture Advertisers (WAMPAS) threw a big party, hosted by the director Fred Niblo, who had been in charge of Rudolph Valentino's great success that year, *Blood and Sand*, and was to direct the silent version of *Ben-Hur* three years later. At the bash, attended by most of Hollywood's great and good, the debut list of 'WAMPAS Baby Stars', young women the organisation thought were headed for the top, was announced. Few of the names mean much today to anyone but devotees of silent cinema. Probably the best known are Bessie Love, who was still appearing in small roles in movies 60 years later, and Colleen Moore, dubbed 'America's Favourite Flapper' at the time. The lists of WAMPAS Baby Stars were issued each year until 1934. Most of the actresses on it are now forgotten but just a few went on to become major stars. Fay Wray, the woman carried off by King Kong in the 1933 film, and Joan Crawford were both WAMPAS Baby Stars of 1926; Ginger Rogers, a couple of years before she teamed up with Fred Astaire, was on the list for 1932.

Flying Down to Rio

Throughout 1922, aviation records of every kind were being broken. Two pilots from the Portuguese navy, Gago Coutinho and Sacadura Cabral, made the first flight across the south Atlantic, travelling the 5,000 miles from Lisbon to Rio de Janeiro in several stages between March and June 1922. They took to the air in a Fairey floatplane on 30 March, hoping to bag a cash prize the Portuguese government had offered to anyone making the first flight between the two cities. Although a landmark flight, their journey was not without major hiccups. They landed at Las Palmas in the Canary Islands without any problems but bad weather forced them to delay their onward journey to the Cape Verde Islands for several days. There, adverse weather conditions once more intervened and it was 17 April before they could take off again. They had already lost the prize – the rules stipulated that the trip should take no more than a week – but they were still determined to make it to Rio.

Their next target was the tiny archipelago known as St Peter and St Paul Rocks, nearly 600 miles off the northern coast of Brazil. It was touch-and-go whether they would be able to locate the islands amidst the ocean vastness. Cabral later wrote that, 'we must have been about 690 miles from the Rocks and we didn't have more than eight and a half hours of fuel left... The logical, the prudent thing to do would have been to turn back, but that would have left a bad impression.' Instead they flew on, and eventually located the archipelago, but, as they struggled to land in heavy seas, their aircraft was damaged and began to sink. A rescue boat had to pick them up and transport them to Fernando de Noronha, an island group nearer the Brazilian coast. There they waited for a replacement plane to be despatched from Portugal.

It arrived on 6 May and the airmen were soon attempting the last stage of their journey. It went disastrously wrong. In a fierce storm, their engines failed and they were obliged to ditch in the ocean. Floating in the water, the plane was immediately surrounded by sharks. 'When they realised that the plane wasn't edible,' Coutinho laconically recalled, 'they went away.' The two men drifted in the ocean currents for nine hours before a British ship rescued them and took them back to Fernando de Noronha. Undeterred, Coutinho and Cabral awaited the arrival of a third plane and resumed their journey on 5 June. Twelve days later, via a series of short hops along the Brazilian coast, they finally arrived in Rio. It had taken them 79 days to make their way there. Of that time they had spent just over 60 hours actually in the air.

Murders in Bavaria

Hinterkaifeck was the name of an isolated farm near Waidhofen in Bavaria. In 1922 it was home to Andreas Gruber and his wife Cäzilia, their widowed daughter Viktoria, their two grandchildren, Cäzilia, aged 7, and Josef, aged 2, and a newly employed maid called Maria Baumgartner. At the end of March 1922, all six inhabitants of the farm were murdered by an unknown attacker (or attackers). They were despatched by repeated blows to the head with a mattock and most of their bodies piled up in the barn. Andreas Gruber was not a popular man in the neighbourhood and his family was severely dysfunctional. He had long been involved in an incestuous relationship with his daughter whose husband had been killed in the First World War. Josef was rumoured to be Andreas's son, although some locals thought the young boy was the product of a relationship between Viktoria and the village mayor, Lorenz Schlittenbauer. The mayor had reportedly offered to marry Viktoria but her tyrannical father had refused to allow it, chasing Schlittenbauer off his property with a scythe when he came to visit.

For some time before the murders, Andreas Gruber had been telling neighbours of strange goings-on at his farm. Livestock had gone missing and he had become convinced that he could hear noises in his attic, as if someone was moving around there. When he went to investigate, he found nothing. Suggestions that he should go to the police had been dismissed. 'I know how to defend myself,' Gruber had said. Events were to prove that he could not have been more wrong.

The bodies of the Gruber family and their maid were not discovered for several days. Although locals thought it curious that none of them had been seen for a while – they didn't attend church as usual – Andreas Gruber's belligerence didn't encourage neighbourly visits. It was not until 4 April that three men, led by Lorenz Schlittenbauer, went to the farm and entered the barn. There they found Andreas, his wife Cäzilia, his daughter and his granddaughter, bludgeoned to death and lying in the hay. The bodies of the boy, Josef, and the unfortunate maid, Maria, who had only arrived to work at Hinterkaifeck the day before the killings, were inside the farmhouse. These discoveries were horrific enough but, in an added touch of the macabre, it seemed that the murderer (s) had remained in the farmhouse for up to seventy-two hours after slaughtering the family. While the corpses were lying in the barn, they had made sure to feed and milk the cows and had helped themselves to food from the pantry.

The police had plenty of suspects, including Lorenz

Schlittenbauer, Viktoria's thwarted suitor, and a persistent housebreaker named Josef Bartl, who had spent time in a mental asylum. Some of them were briefly arrested and then released for want of evidence, and Schlittenbauer, before his death in 1941, took court action against an individual who had described him as 'the Hinterkaifeck murderer'. However, no one was ever brought to trial. The case has never been solved. In Germany, its notoriety continues to this day. Anna Maria Schenkel's novel based on it, *The Murder Farm*, was a bestseller on its publication in 2006 and a film adaptation was released three years later.

The Beautiful and Damned

In the words of the singer and songwriter Hoagy Carmichael, 'The postwar world came in with a bang of bad booze, flappers with bare legs, jangled morals and wild weekends.' In America, no two people exemplified that world more than the young novelist F Scott Fitzgerald and his wife Zelda. Born in St Paul, Minnesota in 1896, Fitzgerald studied at Princeton University but became disillusioned with university life. He dropped out and joined the army, half expecting to be posted to the Flanders trenches. Instead, newly commissioned as a second lieutenant, he was sent to Camp Sheridan near Montgomery, Alabama. In the summer of 1918, he met Zelda Sayre at a country club and was immediately smitten. Nearly four years younger than her future husband, Zelda was born in Montgomery, where her father was a justice of the state's Supreme Court.

The brief verse printed under her high school graduation photograph summed up Zelda's attitude to life at the time and for most of the rest of her days: 'Why should all life be work, when we all can borrow?/Let's think only of today, and not worry about tomorrow.' In a magazine article, Zelda once described the flapper (see also May) as a woman who 'bobbed her hair, put on her choicest pair of earrings and a great deal of audacity and rouge and went into the battle. She flirted because it was fun to flirt.' By this definition, she was herself an archetypal flapper. She was also high-spirited, intelligent and, like her future husband, a writer in the making. (Fitzgerald made much use of her journals in his early fiction and she later wrote *Save Me the Waltz*, a novel published in 1932 which sold poorly at the time but which has gained plenty of admirers in the years since her death.)

Scott Fitzgerald published his first novel, *This Side of Paradise*, in 1920. With a new source of income and the prospect of future fame as a novelist, he was now able to marry Zelda. (Some sources suggest that she had made it a condition of their marriage that her suitor should first prove his worth by getting his book into print.) In March 1922, Fitzgerald's second novel, *The Beautiful and Damned*, was published. (His finest and now most famous work, *The Great Gatsby*, appeared three years later, but it is actually set in the summer of 1922.) A sometimes thinly veiled fictionalisation of his and Zelda's courtship and marriage, *The Beautiful and Damned* did not please all the critics. Described by one as 'blubberingly sentimental', it nonetheless went on to sell 50,000 copies and thrust the couple further into both the literary and the social limelight. As a publicity stunt, Zelda was hired by the *New York Tribune* to write her own review of her husband's book. Unsurprisingly she declared it 'absolutely perfect' and urged the *Tribune*'s readers to buy it so that Scott would have more money to treat her to jewellery and clothes. The Fitzgeralds already had a level of celebrity that few writers and their partners possessed. In the words of the poet and editor Louis Untermeyer, they were 'flaming youth personified'. A double portrait of them was assumed to be instantly recognisable when it was used on the cover of *The Beautiful and Damned* and they were invited to take the starring roles in a movie adaptation even though neither was an actor. (They didn't choose to accept the invitation and the film version featured Marie Prevost and Kenneth Harlan.)

Meanwhile, across the Atlantic in Paris, another young American writer, destined for great acclaim, was just beginning his career. Ernest Hemingway was born in Illinois in 1899 and had worked as a newspaper reporter in Kansas City after leaving high school. At the end of 1917, he had responded to a Red Cross recruitment campaign and signed on to become an ambulance driver in Italy. (His experiences during the First World War, including his period in an Italian hospital, recovering from serious wounds he received in July 1918, later formed the basis of his 1929 novel *A Farewell to Arms*.) After the war had ended he had returned to journalism and settled in Paris where he was a foreign correspondent for the *Toronto Star*. It was in the French capital in July 1922 that Wyndham Lewis encountered Hemingway at Ezra Pound's studio. He was, Lewis reported, 'a splendidly built young man,

stripped to the waist, and with a torso of dazzling white...
He was tall, handsome and serene, and was repelling with
his boxing gloves – I thought without undue exertion – a
hectic assault of Ezra's. After a final swing at the dazzling
solar plexus (parried effortlessly by the trousered statue)
Pound fell back upon his settee.'

'The old and the young,' according to an editorial in the
Atlantic Monthly of October 1922, were 'as far apart in point
of view, code, and standard, as if they belonged to different
races.' The writer went further. 'The two generations
are natural enemies, suspicious of each other, critical,
distrustful, unsympathetic, and hostile.' If Fitzgerald was,
and Hemingway was to become, the idol of a younger
literary generation, then there were other, older writers
whose names meant much to the reading public. Not all of
them still do. Edith Wharton and Willa Cather, who both
published new novels in the year, are considered major
figures in American literature, now even more than they
were then. But who today has heard of Booth Tarkington?
And yet his novel *Alice Adams* won the 1922 Pulitzer Prize
for Fiction. If Tarkington is remembered much at all, it
is probably as the author of *The Magnificent Ambersons*,
published four years earlier, which Orson Welles adapted
as his second Hollywood film in the 1940s.

In retrospect, Fitzgerald and Hemingway appear two
of the giants of American literature in the 1920s. In 1922,
they would not have loomed so large. Fitzgerald, as we
have seen, had been hailed for *The Beautiful and Damned*
and he and his wife were undoubtedly celebrities but *The
Great Gatsby*, the book long acclaimed as his masterpiece,
was three years in the future. Hemingway was almost

entirely unknown outside a small coterie of expatriates in Paris. His first book, the bluntly named *Three Stories and Ten Poems*, was not published until the following year and then only in a privately printed edition of 300 copies. (His writing career was not helped by an incident at the beginning of December 1922 when a valise containing his first novel and most of his other manuscripts was stolen and never recovered.) However, for many Americans who took an intelligent interest in their country's literature, the major publication of the year would probably have been Sinclair Lewis's novel *Babbitt* which appeared in September. A brutally satirical portrait of materialism, complacency and philistinism in Midwestern America, it sold almost three times as many copies as *The Beautiful and Damned*, itself a bestseller. The word 'Babbittry', taken from the novel's central character, George Babbitt, was soon being used to denote mindless conformity and an unthinking adherence to the materialist values of Middle America. Readers were divided between those who thought *Babbitt* a monstrous assault upon ordinary American values and those who thought it a work of genius. Fellow writers were impressed. HG Wells called it 'one of the greatest novels I have read for a long time'; Somerset Maugham thought it a 'complete and rounded work of art'. It was greeted with enthusiasm as far away as Bolshevik Russia where a translation soon appeared. Leon Trotsky told an interviewer that he had found the book 'curiously interesting and instructive though it is too bourgeois in character'. Today Lewis is half forgotten but, in the 1920s, he was routinely described as his country's greatest living novelist. In 1930, he was to become the first American writer to win the Nobel Prize for Literature.

Death of A Novelist's Father

On 28 March, Vladimir Dmitrievich Nabokov, a liberal Russian politician and journalist living in exile in Berlin, was attending a conference at the Philharmonie, a concert hall in that city, at which the main speaker was another exile, Pavel Milyukov, founder of the Constitutional Democratic Party. During proceedings, two far-right, anti-Semitic activists, Pyotr Shabelsky-Bork and Sergey Taboritsky, approached the platform, loudly singing the Tsarist national anthem. Shabelsky- Bork, crying out, 'For the Tsar's family and Russia', fired at Milyukov but missed him. Nabokov, who was sitting near Milyukov, jumped down from the stage and attempted to disarm the would-be assassin. He wrestled his man to the floor but, at this point, the second gunman, Taboritsky, in an attempt to free his associate, turned his weapon on Nabokov. He shot him three times at point blank range. Two bullets hit Nabokov's spine, one passed through his left lung and heart, and he died more or less instantly. Amidst the uproar, as the audience headed for the exits, Taboritsky nearly escaped but a woman bravely shouted, 'Here's the killer' as he passed her and he was captured. So too was Shabelsky-Bork but a further seven members of the audience were wounded in the fracas as the two gunmen fired their weapons indiscriminately.

The dead man's son was the future writer Vladimir

Nabokov, author of *Lolita*, whose fiction includes a number of disguised references to his father's murder. Although he was a student at Trinity College, Cambridge at the time, the younger Nabokov was at the family home in Berlin when he heard the news of his father's death. He accompanied his mother to the Philharmonie, a terrible journey he recalled in a diary entry. 'I looked at the lights swimming past,' he wrote, 'at the whitish bands of lighted pavements... and it seemed to me that I was cut off from this in some fateful manner... and the sole thing clear and significant and alive was the grief, tenacious, suffocating, compressing my heart. "Father is no more." These four words hammered in my brain...'

When the assassins came to trial, it became clear that, eager only to kill Milyukov, they did not even know who Nabokov was. He had simply been in the wrong place at the wrong time and his courage in tackling Shabelsky-Bork had cost him his life. The two gunmen were found guilty and sentenced to 14 years imprisonment but they were released in an amnesty for political prisoners after serving only a few months. Both men later became Nazi collaborators.

April

An air crash over France hits the headlines in Britain
and France but an unknown airman's first flight
over Nebraska will become a more significant date in
aviation history. The last FA Cup Final played before
the opening of the original Wembley Stadium is settled
by a disputed penalty. The last emperor of Austria
dies in exile on the island of Madeira. In America,
President Warren G Harding is in the second year of his
administration. He is a popular figure but he is destined
not to complete it (he will die unexpectedly in July 1923)
and his legacy will be irredeemably tainted by the so-
called 'Teapot Dome' scandal. In China, warlords battle
for control of the vast country. The creator of Sherlock
Holmes, Sir Arthur Conan Doyle, arrives in New York
to bang the drum for spiritualism. The man who may
have been the model for Indiana Jones sets off on an
expedition into the Gobi Desert.

An Air Crash in Picardie

A ir travel was becoming more widespread in the first
years of the decade but its dangers in these early days
were still all too clear. In January 1922, a Handley Page
plane had crashed while approaching Le Bourget airfield
near Paris and the five people on board were killed.
Three months later, the first mid-air collision between
passenger-carrying airplanes occurred. On 7 April, a
British de Havilland DH 18a, with only a pilot and a boy
steward aboard, flew out of Croydon Airport and headed
towards Paris, carrying mail. Some 70 miles north of the
French capital, it entered a bank of fog. Meanwhile, a
plane belonging to the pioneering airline, Compagnie des
Grands Express Aériens, was heading out of Le Bourget
on a regular, daily flight between Paris and London. It
was carrying a pilot, a mechanic and three passengers,
including a honeymooning American couple, Mr and Mrs
Christopher Yule. In the wretched visibility, the two planes
collided above the Picardie countryside and crashed to the
ground. Six people died instantly. The seventh – in some
reports the British pilot, in others the young steward – was
found, badly injured, by rescuers at the scene. He passed
away before he could be taken to hospital.

The Picardie crash was a tragic episode in the early
history of civil aviation and gained headlines in both Britain
and France. In the USA, the *New York Times* reported the
deaths of the honeymooning Americans. However, a more
significant event in the history of aviation took place two
days later, entirely unnoticed by the public, in the skies
above Lincoln, Nebraska. A young man named Charles

Lindbergh made his first flight in an aircraft. He was ecstatic. 'Trees become bushes; barns, toys; cows turn into rabbits as we climb,' he wrote later in his autobiography. 'I lose all conscious connection with the past. I live only in the moment in this strange, unmortal space, crowded with beauty, pierced with danger. The horizon retreats, and veils itself in haze. The great, squared fields of Nebraska become patchwork on a planet's disk.' Five years after his first experience of the delights of taking to the air, Lindbergh made the first non-stop flight from America to Europe, becoming the most famous man in the world as a result and pointing the way towards the transatlantic flights of today.

The Last FA Cup Final before Wembley

The 1922 FA Cup Final was the last to take place before the opening of Wembley Stadium and was played on 29 April at Stamford Bridge, Chelsea FC's ground, between two northern teams – Huddersfield Town and Preston North End. The Huddersfield and Preston final was watched by just over 50,000 spectators and flickering newsreel film footage of it survives. The cameras also rolled at plenty of other sporting events but, in this age of saturation coverage, it's easy to forget that most people followed sport through the newspapers. With no TV, no internet, and radio in its infancy, the press was the main source of information. It was the papers that created the sporting heroes of the day. It was in the pages of the *Daily Mirror*, the *Daily Mail* and all their Fleet Street rivals, as well as local newspapers such as the *Huddersfield Daily Examiner* and the *Lancashire Evening Post*, that fans would have learned what happened at Stamford Bridge.

The last final before Wembley was also the first final to be decided by the award of a penalty. According to those who were there, it was a poor game littered with fouls. 'As a display of football, the game was disappointing,' noted the sports reporter for the *Examiner*, 'for neither side rose to any height of football skill, but the match provided a remarkable display of stamina.' The decisive moment came in the 67th minute when the referee controversially awarded a penalty to Huddersfield. Perhaps unsurprisingly, the man from the *Examiner* thought this was 'justly' given but grainy newsreel footage suggests that Preston were indeed hard done by, and the foul for the penalty was committed outside the box. Billy Smith stepped up to take the kick from the spot, facing the bespectacled Preston goalkeeper Jim Mitchell. (Mitchell, who gained one England cap, may well be the only person to appear in both a Cup Final and an international match while wearing glasses.) He made 'a dashing but fruitless' attempt to save Smith's shot and Huddersfield went on to win 1-0. The manager of the winning side was Herbert Chapman, now a near-legendary figure in the history of football. Chapman had taken over at Huddersfield the previous year and this Cup win was the first major triumph of his career. He went on to win two First Division titles with Huddersfield, two with Arsenal and another FA Cup, and to be acclaimed as the most innovative manager of his era. The next year the final was played at Wembley where chaos ensued when tens of thousands more spectators flooded into the ground than it could hold in the stands. They spilled out on to the pitch and a policeman on a white horse famously had his moment of glory as he endeavoured to clear them so that the match could take place.

Death of a Former Emperor

Karl Franz Joseph Ludwig Hubert Georg Otto Maria, the last Emperor of Austria, the last King of Hungary and the last monarch from the House of Hapsburg before the dissolution of the Austro-Hungarian Empire, died on 1 April, an exile on the Portuguese island of Madeira. After the assassination of Archduke Franz Ferdinand in Sarajevo in 1914, Karl had become the heir presumptive of his great uncle, the Emperor Franz Joseph. When the old man died in 1916, he succeeded him. His reign lasted a little less than two years. Karl attempted to extricate his country from the First World War, making secret peace overtures to the Allies but they all came to nothing, largely because of his refusal to cede any of his territories. This stubbornness proved very short-sighted when the war came to an end and his empire disintegrated.

After peace came in 1918, Karl turned his back on participation in state affairs without actually abdicating and an Austrian Republic was proclaimed. In April 1919, the new Austrian parliament formally stripped him of the throne and he left for Switzerland, escorted by a small guard of British soldiers. Barred from ever returning to Austria, he made two futile attempts to regain the throne of Hungary before being obliged to submit to a more remote exile on Madeira, surrounded by the Atlantic Ocean. There, in March 1922, he caught a cold which developed into pneumonia. Severely ill, he suffered two heart attacks and finally succumbed to respiratory failure. He was 34 years old. His widow, Zita of Bourbon-Parma, never remarried. She wore black in mourning for the rest of her life, finally dying, aged 96, in 1989.

Warren Harding and the Teapot Dome Scandal

In 1922, Warren G Harding was in his second year as the 29th President of the USA. The Republican candidate had swept to office in a landslide in 1920, winning 61 per cent of the popular vote and taking 37 of the 48 states then in the union. Women, voting for the first time in a presidential election, had overwhelmingly cast their votes for him. Warren Gamaliel Harding (his unusual second name was taken from an obscure figure in the Acts of Apostles) was born in Blooming Grove, Ohio in 1865, the son of a doctor, later newspaper owner, and a midwife. After graduating from Ohio Central College, he had followed his father's example and bought a local newspaper, *The Marion Star*. Through a mixture of luck and good management he had succeeded in turning what one biographer called 'a dying rag' into 'a powerful small-town newspaper' and his ambitions had then widened. Entering politics, he had made a steady progress through the ranks of government in his native state. Elected as a state senator in 1900, he had become lieutenant governor of Ohio, effectively deputy to the governor, in 1904. Eleven years later he had headed to Washington as one of the state's two senators in the US Congress.

Harding looked the part of an American president. He was handsome and photogenic. In public he carried himself with the kind of dignified bearing that Americans wanted their national leader to possess. He was affable and easy-going. His presidential campaign slogan had been 'Return to Normalcy' and, in a nation that was undergoing enormous, often unsettling change, the idea of getting back to 'normal' was very appealing. His many liabilities were not so apparent although his political opponents were on hand to point some of them out. The Democrat William McAdoo was, predictably, unimpressed by his powers of oratory. According to McAdoo, the president's speeches 'leave the impression of an army of pompous phrases moving over the landscape in search of an idea; sometimes these meandering words would actually capture a struggling thought and bear it triumphantly, a prisoner in their midst, until it died of servitude and overwork.' Even a professed admirer, the journalist William Allen White, wrote that the president was 'densely ignorant' and given to 'uttering resounding platitudes and saying nothing because he knew nothing.' He was all too likely to listen to whichever person had last spoken to him. White also told the story of Harding speaking to one of his secretaries after an economic debate on the subject of taxation. 'I can't make a damn thing out of this tax problem,' the president confessed. 'I listen to one side and they seem right and then – God! – I talk to the other side and they seem just as right, and here I am where I started.'

The banality of the new president's oratory was

something anyone who listened to his speeches could hear and his intellectual limitations were not unknown. Other aspects of his life, however, were kept well hidden. He was a relentless womaniser. During his campaign for presidency, many of his previous mistresses had been paid off to keep them quiet. However, Harding had no intention of restricting his love life once the election was won. On the night before his inauguration, he had to be persuaded that it would not be a good idea to sneak out of his room in the early hours to meet up with a woman friend. Nan Britton, the mother of Harding's illegitimate daughter, fathered when he was a senator, wrote in a sensational autobiography, published five years after Harding's death, of how their relationship had continued throughout the years of his presidency. On one occasion, she reported, they had had sex in a walk-in wardrobe in the White House.

The president's sex life could, arguably, be described as disreputable but it did little harm to anyone save those closely involved. The same could not be said of his habit of handing out jobs to pals of dubious honesty and even more doubtful morals. The corruption in his administration was on an epic scale. Although some of his appointees were honourable and gifted men – his Treasury Secretary Andrew Mellon went on to serve two more presidents – Harding had a disastrous weakness for old buddies, the so-called 'Ohio Gang', who proved better at backhanders and graft than competent government. Harry M Daugherty, who had known Harding for decades, became Attorney General in the new administration. Daugherty took bribes from bootleggers, gave favours to those willing to pay and diverted government funds into his own bank accounts. He also brought with him to Washington a sidekick named Jess Smith whose wild parties, complete with showgirls brought in from New York, became notorious. Porn films were screened, some of them reputedly featuring actresses who later became well known in less scantily clad roles in Hollywood. At one of these parties a call-girl was accidentally killed when a drink bottle was thrown and struck her on the head. Harding was present and had to be hustled away. The dead girl's brother later made the mistake of trying to blackmail the president. He ended up behind bars.

The biggest example of shady profiteering in Harding's administration only came fully to light after the president's death in 1923 but was in full swing the previous year. It has come to be known as the 'Teapot Dome Scandal'. Before the revelations about Watergate in the 1970s, it was arguably the greatest political scandal in American history. It takes its name from the Teapot Dome Oilfield in Wyoming, one of three such oil-producing areas which a previous president, William Taft, had legally set aside for the needs of the American navy. Taft's idea was that, whatever the emergency, the navy would always have access to oil for fuel. In 1921, Harding had issued an executive order to transfer control of Teapot Dome from the navy to the Department of the Interior which was run by one of his dodgier cronies, a senator from New Mexico named Albert Fall. Fall made illegal arrangements to lease Teapot Dome and another reserve in California to two private oil companies. In return, the companies shovelled nearly half a million dollars and several valuable properties in Fall's direction.

It was in April 1922 that Fall's money-grabbing schemes began to unravel. On the 14th of the month *The Wall Street Journal* reported details of the leasing of Teapot Dome which had hitherto been kept secret. Harding defended Fall, claiming that 'the policy decided upon and the subsequent acts have at all times had my entire approval', but two days after the newspaper revelations a Democratic Senator from Wyoming named John B Kendrick called for an investigation into the Secretary of the Interior's activities. It was the beginning of a series of ever more damaging revelations about the corruption surrounding the Teapot Dome and other oilfields, although it would take years for most of the truth to emerge. In 1927, the Supreme Court ruled that the oilfields had been illegally leased. Fall was finally found guilty of bribery and conspiracy and sent to jail, the first former member of a president's cabinet to be imprisoned for offences committed while he was in office. Harding's presidential legacy was irredeemably tainted.

Warlords in China

In China, the world's most populous nation, the 1920s was a decade of almost continuous conflict, in which warlords fought one another for control of different areas of the vast country. In 1920, two groups, known as the Zhili and the Fengtian cliques, had seized power in Beijing and were thus in nominal charge of the government. Their alliance proved short-lived. Backed by different foreign powers (the Zhili by the British and Americans, the Fengtian by the Japanese), they were bound to fall out. The uneasy coalition had begun to founder in December 1921 when the Fengtian clique replaced the prime minister without consultation. The Zhili clique, angered by this and by the new government's refusal to direct military funds to their troops, forced the replacement prime minister, Liang Shiyi, to resign after only a month in office. Each clique had its own warlord (Wu Peifu on the Zhili side, Zhang Zuolin on the Fengtian's) and political disagreement soon escalated into military confrontation. Troops on both sides were deployed on 10 April and fighting had begun by the end of the month. It lasted for little more than a few weeks. Wu Peifu proved a more astute general than his opponent and the forces of the Fengtian clique were defeated in several engagements. After losing more than 20,000 dead and 40,000 captured, Zhang Zuolin was persuaded to sue for peace. On a British warship anchored off the Chinese coast, representatives of both sides met and a peace treaty was signed. The remaining Fengtian troops headed north to Manchuria, leaving the Zhili in control of Beijing. The peace was not destined to last for very long. A second Zhili-Fengtian War broke out in September 1924 in which the tables were turned and the Fengtian, under new generals, emerged as victors.

Conan Doyle Speaks at Carnegie Hall

After the millions of deaths in the First World War and in the Spanish Flu pandemic, many of those bereaved sought solace in religion. And it was not only the traditional religions that gained new believers. There was a surge in the numbers of those looking for answers in other spiritual movements. Spiritualism itself, with its promises not only of life after death but also the ability of the living to contact loved ones who had 'passed beyond the veil', was given fresh impetus. It had a powerful and very famous advocate in Sir Arthur Conan Doyle, creator of Sherlock Holmes, the world's favourite fictional detective. Doyle had suffered his own grievous losses in recent years. Friends and relatives had died in the war. His much-loved son Kingsley had been badly wounded at the Battle of the Somme but recovered to serve in the army until the middle of 1918. In October of that year, Kingsley had become another victim of the flu pandemic, dying in St Thomas's Hospital, London a few weeks before his 26th birthday.

His father had always been interested in spiritualism – he had joined the British Society for Psychical Research as far back as the 1890s – but now Sir Arthur's commitment to the cause and his belief in the existence of an afterlife grew ever stronger. He was also drawn to other aspects of the supernatural, risking ridicule by lending his support to some dubious claims. In March 1922, Doyle put the finishing touches to his book *The Coming of the Fairies*, published later in the year, which chronicled the curious story of the Yorkshire schoolgirls who, some years earlier, had produced photographs of what they said were fairies living at the bottom of their garden. Although sceptics at the time were scornful and few people today believe anything other than that the 'fairies' were cut out of magazines and prepared for the cameras by the girls themselves, Doyle was adamant that there was something in their story. (It is difficult to understand how he could have been fooled.

Even a cursory glance at the photographs today reveals their artificiality.)

Doyle was by this time a seasoned evangelist for the spiritualist message. A visit to Australia and New Zealand to spread the good news only whetted his appetite for more travels. In 1922, he decided to use a lecture tour to take it to the United States. He and his wife sailed for New York on 2 April, arriving a week later. He was greeted by a horde of reporters and staged an impromptu press conference. According to the *New York Times*, he proclaimed his absolute belief in the afterlife. 'I have talked with and seen twenty of my dead,' he said, 'including my son, when my wife and other witnesses were present... Spiritualism is the one great final antidote to materialism, which is the cause of most of our recent troubles.' Pressed by prurient reporters on the question of whether or not the delights of this world, such as sex and drink, were likely to be accessible in the beyond, he gave it as his opinion that 'certain familiar pleasures' would indeed be available. 'DOYLE SAYS MARITAL RELATIONS OK IN THE NEXT WORLD,' screamed a tabloid headline the following day.

On 12 April, long queues snaked around the streets close to Carnegie Hall. Conan Doyle was due to speak there and gave the first of what were to be several lectures on spiritualism. All were standing room only. The thousands in the audience on that first night included many women wearing a gold star – a sign that they had lost a son during the war. Many of them were awestruck by the lantern slides of spirit phenomena used to illustrate the talk and intensely moved by the sincerity with which Doyle spoke of his own psychic encounters. His account of his meetings with his late mother ('I swear by all that's holy,' he said, 'I looked into her eyes') was greeted with particular enthusiasm.

Much of the newspaper coverage of the event in the days that followed was less sympathetic. Hard-bitten American journalists were disinclined to put much faith in the existence of another world. 'The emotions he excites by the descriptions of visits from the audible and visible dead,' one report said, 'will be... those of pity.' Another suggested that, 'With each of the interviews he gives, it becomes harder to be patient with him.'

The following month, once more at Carnegie Hall, Doyle again illustrated his lecture with a series of 'spirit photographs', including one of editor and campaigning journalist WT Stead who had died when the *Titanic* struck the iceberg a decade earlier. Stead's portrait, according to Doyle, had been obtained by psychic means and had come with a message in the man's handwriting. 'I will try to keep you posted,' Stead had promised from beyond the grave. In all, Doyle gave seven lectures at Carnegie Hall and, after each one, he was mobbed by autograph hunters and well-wishers. Despite the sarcasm of some in the press, he could count his 'spiritualist' tour a success.

It was also during this tour that Doyle had a falling-out with one of his most famous friends. The legendary magician and escapologist Harry Houdini had first met the author two years earlier on a tour of Britain and the unlikely couple had hit it off. In June 1922, Doyle arranged a séance in which his wife Jean, who had a gift for automatic writing, would attempt to contact Houdini's late mother. Although he was deeply sceptical of the claims of spiritualism, Houdini agreed. In Doyle's hotel suite in Atlantic City, Jean was, in her husband's words, 'seized by a spirit'. Supposedly, it was Cecilia Weiss, Houdini's much-loved mother, who had died in 1913. 'It was a singular scene,' Conan Doyle continued, 'my wife with her hand flying wildly, beating the table while she scribbled at a furious rate, I sitting opposite and tearing sheet after sheet from the block as it was filled up, and tossing each across to Houdini, while he sat silent, looking grimmer and paler every moment.' There was little wonder that Houdini was looking grim. He was very far from convinced that the messages were coming from his mother, not least because they were all in English, a language that Cecilia Weiss, who had been born and grown up in Hungary, had barely spoken. His inability to suspend his disbelief caused a rift with Doyle that was unhealed when Houdini died in 1926.

A Real Life Indiana Jones

If there was a model for Indiana Jones, it could well have been Roy Chapman Andrews. Born in Wisconsin in 1884, Andrews had a career that rivalled all but the wilder flights of fantasy in that of the adventurer and archaeologist from the George Lucas films. He began work for the American Museum of Natural History as a very young man and journeyed to a variety of the world's wild places, from the East Indies to the Arctic, in search of specimens for the museum's collections. He had found his metier in life. 'I was born to be an explorer,' he later wrote. 'I couldn't do anything else and be happy... The desire to see new places, to discover new facts – the curiosity of life has always been a resistless driving force in me.' During the First World War he and his wife, the photographer Yvette Borup, spent time in the remoter regions of China in charge of another expedition to hunt down zoological rarities. By 1920, Andrews had become convinced by the now discredited 'Out of Asia' theory of human origins which argued that modern humans first arose not in Africa but in Asia and he was determined to find evidence which would prove it.

Andrews knew Mongolia and its capital city, then known as Ulan Bator, from a visit in 1918. He had found the country fascinating for its 'violent contrasts and glaring anachronisms'. Ulan Bator was, he later wrote, a place where 'motor cars pass camel caravans fresh from the vast, lone spaces of the Gobi Desert' and where 'holy lamas, in robes of flaming red or brilliant yellow, walk side by side with black-gowned priests.' The Gobi Desert was also, he believed, an ideal hunting ground for the kind of traces of ancient humans which would substantiate his theories. He was determined to look for them.

In 1922, he was given the chance and backing from the American Museum of Natural History. He travelled to Beijing to organise an expedition. On 17 April, Andrews and his party left the Chinese capital and set off for Mongolia and the Gobi Desert. Proof of his ideas about human origins turned out to be elusive but the expedition made many important discoveries. Bones of previously unknown prehistoric mammals emerged from the sands. The following year, Andrews's team unearthed the first properly recognised examples of dinosaur eggs. (Giant fossilised eggs had been found in the nineteenth century but they had been mistakenly identified as those of extinct, supersized birds.) In total, Andrews led four further expeditions into the Gobi in the 1920s. His reputation in the years since has sometimes suffered because of his showman's penchant for using the popular bestselling books he wrote to exaggerate both the importance of his findings and the dangers he personally faced in making them. 'Water that was up to our ankles was always up to Roy's neck,' one of his colleagues remarked. However, there is no doubt that he was a very significant figure in the history of palaeontology and our understanding of the ancient past.

May

The cricket season begins in England. In Texas, lynchings and racial violence destroy a small town's reputation. The decade's obsession with speed is reflected in the increasingly competitive struggle to break the land speed record. In London, one of Britain's most flamboyant businessmen and politicians goes on trial for fraud. Kansas City, Missouri becomes the first home of a new animation company. In Russia, the fledgling Bolshevik state faces difficulties as its leader, Vladimir Lenin, suffers a stroke. Although he will survive until January 1924, the battle to succeed him commences. In Weimar, members of an avant-garde art movement conduct its funeral. In Chicago, a small magazine called The Flapper is launched to celebrate the beliefs and activities of a new generation of independent young women. The Lincoln Memorial is dedicated in Washington DC. An attempt to fly around the world ends in failure.

Cricket, Lovely Cricket

The cricket season in England began on 6 May with a number of County Championship matches taking place from Southampton to Manchester. Difficult as it is to credit in this age of non-stop tours and international competitions, the only Test match played in 1922 was not until December when England played South Africa in Johannesburg. (South Africa won by 168 runs.) However, many cricketers whose names are still very familiar to fans of the game a century later were in action during the year. The Surrey and England batsman Jack Hobbs who was the country's most famous cricketer, and 31 years later was to become the first professional player to be knighted, had just returned from a serious illness which had restricted him to five first-class games the previous season. He still finished the 1922 season second in the batting averages with 2,552 runs at an average of 62.24. Ahead of him was Patsy Hendren of Middlesex and England who had scored fewer runs (2,072) but ended with a higher average (66.83). Top of the bowling averages was the veteran Wilfred Rhodes who took 119 wickets at 12.19 runs per wicket. Yorkshire, for whom Rhodes played, were the county champions, winning the title for the first of four successive seasons.

The season included a match which has some claims to being the most remarkable in the history of county cricket. In June, Hampshire played Warwickshire, were bowled out for 15 in their first innings and still won. Warwickshire scored 223 in their first innings and then skittled out the entire Hampshire side in 40 minutes and 8.5 overs. Eight

Hampshire players got ducks. Hampshire were obliged to follow on and their captain, Lionel Tennyson, grandson of the Victorian poet, showed what seemed to be optimism verging on delusion when he told his men, 'Never mind, we'll get 500 this time.' Astonishingly, he was right. When the eighth wicket fell at 274, defeat still looked certain but the last two wickets put on a further 247 runs. Wicketkeeper Walter Livsey, who also happened to be Tennyson's valet, made 110 not out. In their second innings, Warwickshire were bowled out for 158 and Hampshire completed an astonishing comeback. They won by 155 runs.

Lynching in the USA

Throughout the year, vigilante murderers often went unpunished if the killers were white and the victims were black men suspected of crime. Hurley Owen was an African American petty thief, living in Texarkana, Texas who was arrested for stealing car parts. On 19 May, he told the chief of police that, if they let him out of jail, he would lead officers to where his loot was stashed. According to newspaper reports at the time, two policemen accompanied Owen to an alleyway in town where he reached into a dustbin, pulled out a gun he had stored there earlier and ordered his captors to stand back. One of the officers drew his own gun and fired at Owen who was injured but not so badly that he couldn't flee, chased by the police. After the fugitive jumped in a car, Officer Choate tried to prevent him driving off but Owen shot him in the stomach. Choate was taken to hospital where he died

30 minutes later. Owen abandoned the car a mile out of town and, despairing of escape, tried to drown himself in a woodland pond. Dragged from the water he was taken first to hospital, where his wound was dressed, and then to jail. A crowd estimated to be 1,000 strong gathered outside and used a battering ram to break down the doors and seize Owen. With a rope around his neck, he was dragged to a nearby park and killed. His body was then burned.

Probably the worst racial violence of the year in America, however, had occurred in Kirven, Texas a little over a fortnight earlier. On 4 May, Eula Ausley, a 17-year-old white schoolgirl was dragged from her horse near the small township, sexually assaulted and murdered. The discovery of her nearly decapitated body led to a search for her attackers which, despite evidence pointing towards other suspects, soon focused on an African American named McKinley 'Snap' Curry. Taken into custody, Curry, under threats and beatings from the sheriff, pointed the finger at two other black men - Johnny Cornish and Mose Jones. Two days after Eula Ausley's murder, a mob gathered outside the jail where the three suspects were being held. They were hauled out of their cells and burned alive in the centre of Kirven as hundreds watched. 'When one man burned up,' a witness reported, 'they pitched another on the fire, and when that one burned, they threw the third one in the fire.' Even more horrifically, another witness claimed to have seen the three men struggling to crawl from the flames and being driven back into them by onlookers. 'One would wriggle out every once in a while and get thrown back in.'

The terrible deaths of Curry, Cornish and Jones

triggered a month of further racial killings. A few days after the lynching by fire in the town centre, a man named Shadrick Green, friend to two of the victims, was found hanging from a tree. Rumours spread amongst the white population that bands of blacks were forming to take revenge. In reality, it was armed mobs of whites who were the danger. Somewhere between 11 and 23 blacks died at their hands in the next few weeks. By the time the violence came to an end, Kirven's reputation as a pleasant town in which to live was also finished. Nobody was ever convicted of Eula Ausley's murder. Many of the town's black population, fearful for their future, left. So too did some whites. Kirven's prosperity plummeted and it became almost a ghost town.

Feeling the Need for Speed

The 1920s was a decade obsessed by speed. From Olympic athletes to cross-Channel swimmers, from rally drivers to Tour de France cyclists, everyone wanted to go faster, and newspaper readers were only too eager to hear of new records and ever more daring exploits. The land speed record had been held for eight years by a British driver, the splendidly named Lydston Hornsted, who had driven the Blitzen Benz racing car at 124 mph around the Brooklands track in June 1914. On 17 May 1922, Kenelm Lee Guinness, a member of the famous brewing family, climbed into a Sunbeam 350 HP car and set off around the same circuit. Guinness was a man who enjoyed driving quickly at all times. He once told a fellow car enthusiast that the best way to deal with crossroads was to drive across them at high speed because that way you were only in danger of meeting another vehicle for the shortest possible time. Born in 1887, he had first taken an interest in motor racing when he was a Cambridge undergraduate and had driven in Grand Prix races since before the war. 1922 proved his most successful year, and he took the chequered flag in races in Britain, Spain and at Le Mans.

As he roared around the Brooklands track, free from any lingering concerns about crossroads and other traffic, he reached an average top speed of over 133 mph, comfortably breaking Hornsted's record. This was to be the last time that Brooklands was the setting for such a feat, and indeed the last time the record was broken on a closed circuit. A month later, Malcolm Campbell borrowed the car and topped Guinness's speed by 5 mph but, thanks to a dispute over the timing mechanism, this record was never officially recognised. It was not until 1924 that Campbell was finally hailed as 'the fastest man on earth'. By then, he had bought Guinness's car, repainted it blue and called it 'Blue Bird', the name he used for all his record-breaking vehicles and one inspired by the title of a play by the Nobel Prize-winning Belgian writer Maurice Maeterlinck. Guinness's own career ended in tragedy. At the 1924 San Sebastián Grand Prix his car was involved in an accident which injured him severely and killed his mechanic. Guinness never raced again and suffered increasing mental problems. Thirteen years later, he was found dead at his home in what was judged by the coroner to be a suicide.

The Rise and Fall of Horatio Bottomley

Horatio Bottomley was one of the more colourful figures of the age. Born in Bethnal Green, London in 1860, he lost both his parents at a young age and spent a number of formative years in an orphanage before starting work in a solicitor's office. He soon decided that journalism rather than the law provided a better arena for his particular talents. In 1888, he was one of the brains behind the creation of what became the *Financial Times* but some of his endeavours were less legitimate. Throughout the 1890s and 1900s, he demonstrated a gift for dubious money-making schemes which made him a rich man. Despite flirtations with illegality and bankruptcy, Bottomley also enjoyed a political career as a Liberal MP and was the owner of *John Bull*, a populist magazine which had a high circulation and considerable influence during the First World War. In the aftermath of the war, using *John Bull* as his platform, he became the promoter of a drive to buy Victory Bonds, a government-sponsored method of raising cash to bolster the flagging economy. In putting his Victory Bonds scheme into practice, however, Bottomley was none too scrupulous and monies invested in it by ordinary people were diverted to his own use. His downfall began when he antagonised a former associate named Reuben Bigland. In September 1921, Bigland published a pamphlet exposing what he called Bottomley's 'latest and greatest swindle'. Against the advice of his lawyers, Bottomley sued his ex-ally for libel. He lost the case and his own dealings in Victory Bonds were now in the spotlight. His tangled affairs came under police investigation and he was soon facing charges of fraud.

Bottomley's trial began on 19 May 1922. Somewhat surprisingly, the prosecution agreed to a request from Bottomley's defence counsel that there should be a 15-minute adjournment each day so that the MP could drink a pint of champagne which, it was argued, he needed for medicinal purposes. His defence went less well when it came to the actual charges he was facing. Although Bottomley himself informed the members of the jury that the sword of justice would 'drop from its scabbard if you give a verdict of "guilty"', that is exactly what they did. They found him guilty on 23 out of 24 counts. The judge had no doubt that they were correct to do so and did not mince his words when he addressed Bottomley. 'You have been rightly convicted... of this long series of heartless frauds,' he told the MP. 'The crime is aggravated by your high position, by the number and poverty of your victims, by the trust which they reposed in you. It is aggravated by the magnitude of your frauds and by the callous effrontery by which they were committed.' He sentenced Bottomley to seven years' penal servitude. An appeal was rejected and Bottomley found himself persona non grata in the House of Commons. He was expelled as an MP. Released in 1927, he attempted a comeback but his day was done. According to a biographer, he was 'a broken old man' who 'stumbled into obscurity' in his last years, dying of a stroke in 1933.

Laugh-O-gram Films

On 23 May, a major event in the history of American cinema took place in Kansas City, Missouri, largely unnoticed by the wider world. A young animator incorporated his first production company which he called Laugh-O-gram Films. It was not an immediate financial success and its 21-year-old chief ended the year living in the Laugh-O-gram office because he couldn't afford more luxurious accommodation. He had, however, produced a number of short, black-and-white films based on familiar fairy tales, beginning with *Little Red Riding Hood*. The animator's name was Walt Disney.

Although born in Chicago, Disney had lived in Kansas City as a boy, only returning to his native city in 1917 when he took courses at the Chicago Academy of Fine Arts. After a period in France, working as an ambulance driver for the Red Cross, he moved back to Kansas City, intent on forging a career as a cartoonist. Working at the Pesmen-Rubin Commercial Art Studio, he made friends with another young artist named Ub Iwerks and the two set up their own studio in 1920. It struggled to make money and Disney and Iwerks were obliged to join the Kansas City Film Ad Company where they both became fascinated by the potential of the fledgling art of film animation.

In 1921, Disney approached the Newman Theatre in Kansas City, with a sample animation reel. The manager of Newman's liked what he saw and commissioned the young animator to make a series of short cartoons which were to be called Newman's Laugh-O-grams. The following year, Disney used what few assets remained from the company he had set up with Ub Iwerks, plus an extra $15,000 from other investors, to create Laugh-O-gram Films. Iwerks and other men, such as Hugh

Harman and Friz Freleng who went on to storied careers in American animation, joined him in creating twelve cartoons based on fairy tales. As well as *Little Red Riding Hood*, others which survive include *Puss in Boots*, *Cinderella* and *The Four Musicians of Bremen*. Unfortunately, the contract Disney had signed with Newman's manager was much better value for the movie theatre than it was for Laugh-O-gram. By the summer of 1923, the company was in deep financial trouble. Clutching the reels of the last film made at the studio (a mixture of live-action and animation entitled *Alice's Wonderland*), Disney headed for Hollywood to try his luck there.

In later years, Disney told the story that Mickey Mouse owed his inspiration to a mouse that used to visit him at the Laugh-O-gram studio. He had put it in a cage on his desk and grown particularly fond of it. 'By tapping him on the nose with my pencil, I trained him to run inside a black circle I drew on my drawing board. When I left Kansas City... I hated to leave him behind. So I carefully carried him to a backyard, making sure it was a nice neighbourhood, and the tame little fellow scampered to safety.' Five years later, the memories of his pet mouse in Kansas City were behind the creation of the most iconic character in the history of animation. Whether or not Disney's tale is true – and it does sound more apocryphal than entirely accurate – there is no doubt that the Laugh-O-gram films were important in the trajectory of his own career. Without them, there would probably have been no Walt Disney Studios, and the American media industry would look very different.

Lenin Declines

In 1918, Lenin had been the victim of an assassination attempt by a twenty-eight-year-old woman named Fanny Kaplan who believed that he was betraying the Revolution by turning Russia into a one-party state. The Bolshevik leader had been giving a speech at the Hammer and Sickle factory in Moscow. As he left the building and walked towards his car, he was approached by Kaplan who fired three shots. One missed its target. The other two lodged in his shoulder and neck. In 1922, the bullets were still there. A German doctor named Burkhardt, who had argued that Lenin's increasingly terrible headaches were the result of lead poisoning from these shells, was given the go-ahead for an operation to remove one of them in April. Under local anaesthetic, the operation was a success, Lenin enduring the considerable discomfort with quiet stoicism. However, his health continued to be a cause for concern. On 26 May, he suffered a stroke. He was all but paralysed down his right side and was, for a time, incapable of speech. In great mental and physical distress, he contemplated suicide. At one point, Lenin's wife, Natalia Krupskaya, intended to feed him cyanide but could not bring herself to do so. Instead the couple approached Stalin, a 'steely man devoid of sentimentality', asking him to provide Lenin with poison. Stalin refused. For the moment, he wanted Lenin alive.

With Lenin incapacitated for part of 1922, the question of who should be his successor became unavoidable. Lenin himself thought that the ideal solution would be a collective leadership once he had died but, in reality, it became increasingly clear that there were only two main contenders to replace him – Trotsky and Stalin. The latter had already manoeuvred himself into a strong position when he was appointed General Secretary of the Communist Party on 3 April. Now he worked hard to isolate the often wheelchair-bound Lenin from other leading Bolsheviks and he began to promote his own supporters and friends into key positions in the party apparatus. Soon thousands of officials throughout the country owed their careers to Stalin.

Throughout the summer of 1922, Russia was, in effect, ruled by three men united only by their opposition to Trotsky. Although he was Trotsky's brother-in-law, Lev Kamenev had his own ambitions to become leader and thought they were best served by opposing the man he considered his most serious rival. Grigory Zinoviev had long loathed Trotsky. In the words of the historian Orlando Figes, 'he would have sided with the Devil so long as it secured his enemy's defeat'. As events unfolded, it turned out that Kamenev and Zinoviev might as well have sided with the Devil when they formed a triumvirate with Joseph Stalin. They thought they were using him; the truth was that he was using them. Fourteen years later they were to pay for their mistake with their lives when they both became leading victims of the Moscow Show Trials of the 1930s.

Lenin returned to work in September but soon realised that Stalin and his two temporary allies were intent on sidelining him. Because he had not fully recovered from his stroke, he often left Politburo meetings early, only learning later that important decisions had been made in his absence. In October, his suspicions were further aroused by Stalin's proposal that Trotsky should be expelled from the Politburo. In mid-December, Lenin suffered another stroke. Stalin moved quickly to isolate him during his recuperation. Visitors were severely restricted and correspondence monitored. According to an order from the Politburo, 'Neither friends nor those around him are allowed to tell Vladimir Ilich any political news, since this might cause him to reflect and get excited.' Despite the effects of the stroke, Lenin was soon all too aware of what was happening. 'I have not died yet,' he told his sister, 'but, led by Stalin, they have already buried me.'

By the very end of the year, as he struggled with his deteriorating health, he was beginning to understand just how awful the prospect of Stalin's succession was. In what became known as 'the 1922 documents', dictated to a secretary, he set out to warn his Bolshevik colleagues of the dangers he foresaw. Stalin, he thought was 'too coarse' and had defects which were 'intolerable in a General Secretary'. It was time for the comrades to 'think about a way to remove Stalin from that post' and replace him with someone who would show 'greater tolerance, greater loyalty, greater courtesy and consideration to comrades, less capriciousness.' The 1922 documents were supposed to be kept secret from Stalin but, unfortunately, Lenin was surrounded by spies. Both of his main secretaries reported back to the Georgian. One of them, Nadezhda Alliluyeva, was actually Stalin's wife. Lenin's attempts to put the genie of Stalin back in the bottle were doomed. The Soviet leader had a third stroke, in March of the following year, which robbed him of his ability to speak. He died in January

1924. By that time, Stalin was well on the way to gaining the supreme, murderous power he was to exercise until his own death nearly three decades later.

Dada Dies

On 22 May, members of an avant-garde art movement attended a festival at the Bauhaus school in Weimar where they staged a mock funeral. The artists and writers were Dadaists and the death rites they were conducting were for their own movement. One of Dada's most prominent figures, the Romanian poet, Tristan Tzara, had proclaimed that, 'Dada is useless, like everything else in life...' Now his fellow Dadaists were intent on ending its useless existence.

Dada, like so much of the cultural life of the 1920s, had its origins in the First World War. First emerging in 1916 in the Cabaret Voltaire, a nightclub in Zurich where the artistic avant-garde gathered, it was a rejection of a civilisation which had led, in the minds of the original Dadaists, to nothing more than the slaughter in the trenches. Dada – the name, in one oft-repeated story, was chosen by the German artist Richard Huelsenbeck when he opened a dictionary at random and came across a French colloquialism for 'hobby-horse' – was defiantly 'anti-art'. Its leading members, such as Tzara, the sculptor Jean Arp and the German writer Hugo Ball, rejected reason and logic in favour of nonsense and irrationality. From Zurich, Dada spread through Europe. Groups formed in Berlin, Cologne, in the Netherlands and in Romania. Across the Atlantic, American artists like Man Ray and

European exiles such as the enigmatic painter and pioneer of conceptual art Marcel Duchamp put New York on the Dada map.

In France, the ill-defined movement attracted the support of the poet and one-time Cubist painter Francis Picabia and of younger writers, many of them scarred by their experiences in the war, such as André Breton, Louis Aragon and Philippe Soupault. For the next few years, Dadaism was at the very cutting edge of the European avant-garde but, by 1922, it was slowly expiring. In the words of one critic, writing particularly about Paris Dada, it 'had become mired in its own negativity'. In its prolonged death throes, it was slowly giving birth to a movement that was to have a far more profound and lasting impact on the arts of the next century – Surrealism.

Several months before the Weimar funeral, Breton, the future 'Pope of Surrealism', had declared war on the Dadaism to which he had previously been committed and on Tzara, his one-time ally, by organising what he called the 'Congress for the Determination and Defence of the Modern Spirit'. In a heated meeting at the Closerie des Lilas, a bar and restaurant popular with Parisian intellectuals, tempers ran high. Breton had already proclaimed Tzara a 'publicity-mongering imposter' and now the two men and their supporters nearly came to blows. Battle lines were drawn and the Paris Dadaists divided into two opposing camps. The first Surrealist Manifesto was still two years in the future but, when Breton went on to publish a statement entitled 'After Dada', the seeds of a new movement were sown.

The Flapper

In May, a new magazine was published in Chicago. It was called *The Flapper* and it advertised itself on its masthead as 'Not for Old Fogies'. On its very first page its editors announced their philosophy of life. 'Greetings, flappers!' they wrote. 'All ye who have faith in this world and its people, who do not think we are going to the eternal bowwows, who love life and joy and laughter and pretty clothes and good times, and who are not afraid of reformers, conformers, or chloroformers – greetings!...Thanks to the flappers the world is going round instead of crooked, and life is still bearable. Long may the tribe wave!'

The word 'flapper' had been around for decades. In the 1890s it had been used derogatorily to refer to a young prostitute. By 1904, and its use in *Sandford of Merton*, a novel about Oxford life ('There's a stunning flapper,' one of his characters remarks), it had lost its disparaging connotations and simply meant an attractive young woman. It was only after the First World War that the word began to be applied to a specific generation of young women with specific attitudes to life. The war had undermined people's beliefs in old orthodoxies and assumptions. Younger women, in particular, wanted freedoms that the previous generation hadn't imagined possible. Most of all, they wanted the freedom to enjoy themselves. A Hollywood film of 1920 simply entitled *The Flapper* introduced the life of the flapper to a wider audience and, by 1922 and the launch of the Chicago magazine, she had become an iconic figure of the Roaring Twenties.

Unsurprisingly, assorted arbiters of morality were swift

to condemn the flapper. An American politician went on record to censure 'the flippancy of the cigarette-smoking, cocktail-drinking flapper'. A Harvard psychologist gave his opinion that flappers were notable for 'the lowest degree of intelligence'. The truth is that many people found flappers threatening. They were women who refused to behave as the critics believed women should. They went out and about without chaperones. They danced suggestively, dressed provocatively and enjoyed flirting (and more) with young men. As the American historian Susan Ferentinos puts it, 'Flappers prized style over substance, novelty over tradition, and pleasure over virtue.' Perhaps most damningly of all, they refused to take the male sex as seriously as many men took themselves. 'It is the purpose of *The Flapper*,' one contributor to the magazine wrote, 'to find out whether or not there is room for improvement in the so-called lord of creation – whether all the blame for extremes in behaviour deserves to be centred on the flapper, or whether it can be traced to the male of the species to whose whims she is supposed to constantly cater.'

Lincoln Remembered

There had been talk of a national monument to Abraham Lincoln ever since the immediate aftermath of his assassination. As early as 1867, a sculptor named Clark Mills had been commissioned to create a fitting tribute and had come up with a design for a large structure, topped by a twice-life-size statue of the murdered president. Plans had to be abandoned when a subscription fund was unable to raise the money necessary to build it. Further schemes at the beginning of the twentieth century were viewed with scepticism by some politicians and several bills proposing them failed to pass Congress. It was not until 1910 that one succeeded and the Lincoln Memorial Commission, with the then president, William Taft, at its head, was brought into being. A site was chosen, and the design – for a neoclassical, temple-like structure with a colossal statue of Lincoln inside – agreed upon. In February 1914, the project was officially initiated, and building work began the following month. After more than eight years, the Lincoln Memorial was finally dedicated in a ceremony which took place on 30 May 1922.

Amongst those attending this ceremony was Robert Todd Lincoln, the assassinated president's eldest son and the only one to survive into adulthood. He was 78 years old and had himself had a distinguished career as a lawyer, politician and diplomat, including a period as US Ambassador to the Court of St James's (i.e. to Britain). He was breaking a habit of 20 years by attending. Robert Todd Lincoln had been coincidentally present or nearby when all three of the American presidents so far assassinated had been killed. Although he did not go to Ford's Theatre on the night his father was shot, he had joined the fatally wounded Abraham Lincoln at his deathbed. In 1881, Robert Lincoln was at the Washington train station when James Garfield was shot; in 1901, he was invited by President McKinley to the Pan-American Exposition in Buffalo and was just outside the building when the anarchist Leon Czolgosz fired his gun at McKinley who died a week later. Robert Lincoln developed a superstitious belief that he was a bad omen for presidents, reportedly refusing another invitation with the words, 'No, I'm not going... because there is a certain fatality about presidential functions when I am present.'

On this occasion, however, Robert Lincoln was there to hear a succession of speakers extol his father's achievements. The poet Edwin Markham read out his poem 'Lincoln, the Man of the People'. The only black speaker, Robert Russa Moton, was the son of former slaves from Virginia. The formal dedication of the memorial was carried out by former president William Taft, now the Chief Justice of the Supreme Court who called Lincoln 'the nation's saviour'. Present president Warren Harding gave an address which raised more than a few eyebrows. Although, unsurprisingly, he bestowed glowing praise on Lincoln for 'his wisdom, his unselfishness, his sublime patience' and 'the sheer greatness of his intellect', he also claimed, in what seemed almost a throwaway remark early in his speech, he 'would have compromised with the slavery that existed, if he could have halted its extension.'

Such an attitude may not have come as much of a surprise to Moton and the handful of other prominent African Americans who had been invited to witness the dedication of this memorial to the president who had freed black slaves. They found that they were directed to a separated, roped-off enclosure. One of the US Marines guarding this segregated section supposedly gestured to one man and said, 'Niggers over here.'

Failing to Fly Round the World

New uses for the aeroplane were being found. At the Epsom Derby on 31 May 1922, an RAF pilot named Cyril Turner flew above the crowds and used skywriting to spell out 'Daily Mail' in a bid to persuade racegoers to buy the paper. Other attempts at aerial firsts proved too ambitious. A week previously, Major Wilfred Blake had embarked on a mission, sponsored by a national newspaper, to fly around the world. (In April, an earlier plan to circle the globe in a Vickers Viking amphibious aircraft had been abandoned after the chief pilot, Sir Ross Smith, crashed near Weybridge and was killed during a trial flight.) Together with an experienced pilot, Norman Macmillan, and the filmmaker Geoffrey Malins, brought in to make a movie about the adventure, Blake set off from Croydon Aerodrome in a de Havilland DH 9 on 24 May. His idea was to use several different planes to make the journey in four stages.

The first part of the plan did not get off to a brilliant start. To one onlooker, their plane looked 'extremely small and frail for such an ambitious flight' and they had only reached the south of France when Macmillan was obliged to make a forced landing near Marseille which damaged the DH 9's undercarriage and wrecked its propeller. Stranded for several weeks, Blake grew ever more frustrated and eventually he ordered another plane to be sent from England. It was well into June before they were back in the air. Further problems followed over Italy. In the words of Macmillan, as they approached the aerodrome at Brindisi on a scheduled stop, 'a deep ditch, completely hidden in the long grass, tripped us up at the very end of the landing run'. While waiting for repairs, the pilot injured his foot in an automobile accident and was obliged to fly the next stage wearing carpet slippers.

After a rest in Athens, where Macmillan recovered enough to resume ordinary footwear, the aerial adventurers journeyed, via Crete and Egypt, to Palestine. Their trip across the Syrian Desert to Baghdad was enlivened by encounters with tribesmen who shot at their plane as they passed overhead. By 17 July, they were in Karachi and were soon zigzagging their way back and forth across the Indian subcontinent. It was here that everything really began to unravel. Blake himself had to pull out, suffering from appendicitis. Macmillan and Malins, swapping their old aircraft for a new one, flew on but it was monsoon time and scarcely the kind of weather suitable for a flimsy biplane. On 22 August, their new plane experienced engine trouble and plummeted into the Bay of Bengal. The two men floated for two days and nights before they were rescued from their slowly capsizing aircraft. 'They were in a very bad state,' one of their rescuers remembered, 'and almost exhausted, tongues swollen and skins turned black by the sun, and their feet so badly swollen from salt water that they could scarcely walk, and both had high fever.' The attempt to circle the world was abandoned. 'It was foredoomed to failure', *Aeroplane* magazine sniffily reported but it had been a valiant effort.

June

A book of verse provides a low-key beginning to the career of one of the twentieth-century's bestselling authors. An American golfer wins the British Open for the first time. In Ireland attempts to end the occupation of the Four Courts in Dublin by republicans implacably opposed to the treaty signed at the end of the previous year between the British government and Irish nationalists mark the outbreak of civil war. In the USA, labour troubles hit the country badly. Disputes in the railroad and mining industries lead to widespread strikes and unrest, some of which result in terrible violence. In Germany, the Weimar regime struggles for stability and is rocked by the assassination of its foreign minister. Japan withdraws its troops from Siberia.

JUNE

Firsts in Children's Literature

In June 1922, a publisher named J Saville & Co. Ltd produced a small book of children's verse entitled *Child Whispers*. It attracted some favourable attention but nobody could have guessed that it was the launch of probably the most successful career in children's literature. *Child Whispers* was Enid Blyton's first published book. Over the next 46 years, until her death in 1968, Blyton produced hundreds of books featuring such characters as the Famous Five, Noddy and the Secret Seven. More than 600 million copies of them have been sold and she has been translated into nearly 100 languages. Despite the controversy surrounding her work, both in her lifetime and, increasingly, in the decades since her death – she has been variously accused of racism, xenophobia, sexism and a multitude of other sins – she continues to attract young readers in large numbers.

1922 proved to be a good year for children's literature. In Britain, it saw the first in a series of books by a Lancashire-born classics teacher called Richmal Crompton. *Just William*, chronicling the adventures of William Brown, a scruffy, anarchic schoolboy whose well-meaning plans always led him into disaster, was published by George Newnes Ltd. It was followed by 38 other William books and the character has been regularly portrayed in films, on radio and in TV series over the years. In America, Margery Williams created a lasting classic in *The Velveteen Rabbit*, the story of a toy rabbit that yearned to become real. 1922 was also the year in which the Newbery Medal, the most prestigious prize in American children's literature, was first awarded. Named after John Newbery, an eighteenth-century London publisher who was one of the earliest to concentrate on children's books, it went to *The Story of Mankind*, an impeccably educational account of world history for young readers by the Dutch-American writer Hendrik Willem van Loon. Van Loon's book is still in print today, its latest revision taking in events of the 2010s.

Walter Hagen Wins the British Open

For the first 62 years of its existence no golfer born in the United States won the British Open. This all changed on 23 June 1922 when, at the Royal St George's Golf Club in Kent, Walter Charles Hagen became the first native-born American to win the prestigious 'Claret Jug'. (The winner in the previous year, Jock Hutchison, lived and played his golf in the USA, but, as his name strongly suggested, had been born and raised in Scotland.) Hagen was undeniably American. He had come into the world in the city of Rochester, New York State in 1892, and had celebrated his first victory in the US Open aged only 21. He arrived to compete for the British Open for the first time in 1920 and made the mistake of registering himself as WC Hagen. Every time his name and score were posted, the British crowds, primed to associate the letters 'WC' mainly with the toilet, laughed. Baffled and irritated, Hagen finished 53rd, more than 25 strokes behind the winner. Two years later, the crowds were cheering rather than laughing as he snatched victory by one stroke from his rivals, Jim Barnes and George Duncan. Although, as one American newspaper put it at the time, the British had been forced into 'swallowing the bitterest golf pill they have ever known', spectators took to the affable and self-confident Hagen.

He went on to win the British Open three more times in the 1920s and to become, like Jack Dempsey and Babe Ruth, one of the decade's sporting superstars. He earned, for the time, prodigious amounts of money and wasted no time in spending it. 'I never wanted to be a millionaire,' he once said. 'I just wanted to live like one.' Hagen certainly had a taste for the high life. He dressed smartly (his silk shirts were shipped specially from Japan and his shoes hand-made in London), always travelled first class, and owned a series of high-powered cars. Despite his successes, he was never an enthusiast for overdoing training and practice. 'Eighteen holes a day is enough for anyone to play,' he once said. A showman both on and off the course, he played hundreds of exhibition matches in his career and regularly joined celebrity friends for photo ops. He was no great respecter of rank. The story that he broke royal etiquette while playing a round with the Prince of Wales (later Edward VIII) by cheerily ordering his opponent to 'Pull the pin, Eddie' when they approached the green is probably apocryphal but it is true that he once kept President Warren Harding waiting at the first tee because he hadn't finished shaving to his satisfaction. Hagen, although his fame has faded, has been described as one of the most important figures in the history of his sport. Bernard Darwin, long-time golf correspondent for The Times, summed up his secret as succinctly as anyone. 'The difference between Hagen and other players,' he once wrote, 'is that he just wins and they just don't.'

Fighting in the Streets of Dublin

The Anglo-Irish Treaty was signed on 6 December 1921, bringing to an end the Irish War of Independence. In London, the Prime Minister, Lloyd George, had manoeuvred the Irish negotiators, including Michael Collins and Arthur Griffith, into a difficult position. He had insisted that they sign the Treaty without giving them proper time to refer its provisions back to colleagues in Dublin. He had also waved the possibility of renewed war in front of their noses in order to concentrate their minds. In the circumstances, the Irish negotiators had felt that they had no option but to sign. Collins, who had been one of the leading figures in the negotiations on the Irish side, thought that the treaty to which he had signed his name was the best that was on offer at the time. It was a 'stepping stone' and gave Ireland, he claimed, 'the freedom to achieve freedom'.

Almost immediately, however, the Treaty was rejected by a significant sector of the republican movement. Some of its provisions proved unacceptable to many nationalists. Every nationalist group – from the members of the Dáil, the Irish parliament, to the IRA – was split. Most obviously, the fact that the six counties of Northern Ireland were to remain in the United Kingdom was a bitter blow to those who wanted a free, whole and united Ireland. And the Irish Free State, established by the Treaty, was to remain a British Dominion, with George V as its monarch, anathema to the most committed republicans. To them, too many of the trappings of imperialism would remain. The political leaders of the fight for independence were themselves divided. Eamon De Valera, the man who had, in his role as president of the nascent Republic, actually granted the Irish delegates to the talks the authority to negotiate and conclude a deal, now opposed it. 'The whole of Ireland will not get me to be a national apostate,' he said on 6 January, 'and I am not going to connive at setting up in Ireland another government for England.'

As a new year dawned, the seeds of civil war had been sown. Although the Dáil voted on 7 January 1922, by the narrow margin of 64 to 57, in favour of the Treaty, too many nationalists were implacably opposed to it. Two days later, De Valera resigned as president and was replaced by Arthur Griffith. A week later British rule officially ended and troops began to be withdrawn. The country was now dangerously divided between those in favour of the treaty and those against it. A Provisional Government was set up, while the legislation creating the Free State was going through the British parliament and the Dáil, but its members were in an unenviable position. In the memorable words of one commentator, they were 'standing amidst the ruins of one administration, with the foundations of another not yet laid, and with wild men screaming through the keyhole.'

In a speech at Killarney, de Valera said that, if the Treaty were accepted, IRA men would have 'to wade through Irish blood, through the blood of the soldiers of the Irish government, and through, perhaps, the blood of some of the members of the government in order to get Irish freedom'. He claimed that he meant his words to be a warning of the possibility of civil war but, to many, they sounded more like an incitement to it. Michael Collins called this and similar speeches 'the language of madness' but the rhetoric and the violence were both growing wilder. The anti-Treaty IRA were accumulating arms and explosives. Money was seized in raids on more than 300 post offices in the first weeks of April.

In June, elections to the Dáil were held. Of the 128 seats, 92 went to pro-Treaty candidates but, far from settling the issue, the election proved the prologue to the violence of civil war. Since April, a large group of IRA men, led by Rory O'Connor, had been occupying the Four Courts buildings in Dublin, an elegant Georgian complex that was the centre of the Irish legal system. In the words of one of them, Ernie O'Malley, they had 'barricaded the windows with heavy legal tomes, weighty ledgers and tin boxes filled with earth.' The Public Record Office was turned into an ad hoc munitions factory, making mines and grenades. Their intentionally provocative actions failed to result in the retaliation they both expected and wanted, and Michael Collins and others strove desperately to persuade them to leave. In the aftermath of the assassination of Sir Henry Wilson (see page 126), and following the kidnapping of 'Ginger' O'Connell, a general in the Free State Army, their patience ran out. They were also facing intense pressure from Lloyd George and the British government who believed that they 'had a right to expect that the necessary action towards the occupants of the Four Courts would be taken without delay.' In the early morning hours of 28

June, the Provisional Government forces began shelling the Four Courts. Further demands to surrender were delivered to the occupiers but O'Connor was defiant. 'The boys here... will fight for the Republic to the end,' he wrote in a statement that was smuggled out of the Four Courts at the end of the first day's fighting. 'Will our misguided former comrades outside attack those who stand for Ireland alone?' The answer to his question was, 'Yes, they would.' Although Collins was extremely unwilling to fight against men he called friends, he believed he had no choice.

On the morning of 30 June a temporary truce was called so that the wounded could be evacuated but renewed shelling in the afternoon sparked a large explosion in the Irish Public Record Office, part of the Four Courts complex, which was being used as an ammunition store. Irish state records, some dating back eight centuries, were destroyed in the blast and a mushroom cloud of smoke rose 200 feet in the Dublin sky. At about 4 in the afternoon, the anti-Treaty garrison surrendered and Rory O'Connor and most of his men were taken prisoner.

Over the course of the next week, the streets of Dublin saw a series of running battles. The focus of the fighting was O'Connell Street where Oscar Traynor led a small unit of anti-Treaty IRA men who had commandeered a group of buildings, including several hotels, and had connected them into a stronghold by tunnelling through the walls. On 5 July, with most of the buildings they held on fire, Traynor and the majority of his fighters escaped, mingling with civilians in the street. Cathal Brugha, who had been Minister of Defence in the earlier Irish government but had declared himself an implacable opponent of the

Treaty, together with a small rearguard, was left behind in the Hammam Hotel. In the late afternoon, Brugha ordered his men to surrender but refused to do so himself. He later emerged from the hotel and approached the Free State troops, holding a revolver. One of them shot him in the leg, severing a major artery. He died two days later. Serious fighting in Dublin was effectively over, although the war continued beyond the capital.

The Herrin Massacre, Strikes and the Daugherty Injunction

Violent disputes characterised industrial relations throughout the USA in 1922. The worst of them unfolded in the small mining town of Herrin, Illinois, where a strike led to mob brutality and the loss of 23 lives. A national coal strike had begun in April and, by June, its effects were beginning to bite. In Herrin, the owner of the Southern Illinois Coal Company had originally reached an accommodation with the strikers but he now turned to scab labour, recruited by agencies in Chicago, to move his coal to market. He also employed private guards to protect the strike breakers. The striking miners, mostly members of the United Mine Workers union, were outraged. Tensions began to rise. The mine superintendent, CK McDowell, was heard making inflammatory remarks. 'We came down here to work this mine, union or no union,' he said. 'We will work it with blood if necessary.' It was becoming clear that it would be necessary. On 21 June, a confrontation resulted in an exchange of gunfire and deaths on both sides. Strikers, some of whom had travelled from other parts of the state, now surrounded the Southern Illinois Coal Company mine near Herrin and demanded that the strike breakers stop work. Realising that they were outnumbered, the scab labourers agreed to do so, provided they were given safe passage out of the area. Terms were agreed and 50 or 60 strike breakers emerged from the mine with their hands raised in surrender.

Together with McDowell, they were herded together and the miners began to march them back towards Herrin, five miles away. En route the mob of union supporters grew in numbers and unruliness. The strike breakers were verbally threatened ('the only way to free the county of strike breakers is to kill them all off,' one miner called out) and beaten with the butts of rifles. McDowell was a particular target. He was soon bleeding from several wounds to the head. Although he was elderly and disabled, he got little sympathy. 'We ought to hang that old peg-legged son-of-a-bitch,' one union man shouted. McDowell fell several times and was forced back to his feet. Eventually, he was led off down a side road and shots were heard. His body, with two bullets in his chest, was later found by a farmer in his field. As the forced march towards Herrin continued, the crowds of miners and their allies lost whatever discipline they had once possessed. Some strike breakers had already been killed. In another field, the survivors were lined up against a barbed-wire fence and told to run for their lives. 'Let's see how fast you can run between here and Chicago, you damned gutter-bums,' one miner is reported to have shouted. Union men shot at them as they broke through the fence and fled into nearby woods. One of the guards, a man named Edward Rose, decided that his best chance was to play dead. He heard one of the miners yell, 'By God. Some of 'em are breathing. They're hell to kill, ain't they?' The man then shot him in the back. Rose was wounded but survived. Others were not so lucky.

Six of the strike breakers were captured and taken into Herrin. Surrounded by a crowd of several hundred men, women and children, who beat and kicked them, they were driven towards the town cemetery. There they were yoked together with a rope. A volley of pistol shots was fired and the bound men fell to the ground. Further shots were fired. When it was clear that three of the stricken men were still alive, their throats were slashed with a pocket-knife. Indignities were heaped upon the bodies of strike breakers. At the cemetery, one man was seen urinating in the faces of the dead. Nobody stopped him. Later, after some kind of order had been restored, the wounded were taken to hospital. The dead were despatched to a storeroom in Herrin. There they were stripped, washed and put on public display for several hours. Miners with their families filed past them. Some spat on the corpses which were partially covered by thin sheets. One woman, her children in tow, is alleged to have said, 'Look at the dirty bums who tried to take the bread out of your mouths.'

The shocking events in Herrin were the culmination of one of the worst disputes in a year of regular confrontations between employers and employees throughout the nation. The following month saw railroad workers from several unions come out on strike. Around 400,000 downed tools, either literally or metaphorically, and walked away from their jobs on July 1. Just as the mine owners had done in the coal strike, the railroad companies retaliated by hiring strike breakers and armed guards to protect them. Again one of the inevitable consequences was violence. Unlike the events in Herrin, this was mostly directed at the strikers themselves. From Port Morris, New Jersey to Needles, California, there were incidents in which guards opened fire on striking workers. In Wilmington, North Carolina, a 'special guard' on the Atlantic Coast Line Railroad took such exception to being called a scab by an engineer named HJ Southwell that he shot him dead. With cruel irony, Southwell was not actually on strike himself. In the city of Buffalo in New York State, railroad detectives accidentally gunned down a woman and two children.

There was little doubt whose side the federal government was on. Harry M Daugherty, Attorney General in Warren Harding's administration, was a bitter opponent of union power and quick to see wicked forces at play in the strike. 'Here indeed was a conspiracy worthy of Lenin,' he remarked with a paranoid conviction that Bolsheviks were intent on undermining American industry and he proved more than willing to offer government assistance to the railroads. Federal marshals could frequently be found in the ranks of those breaking up the strikes and forcefully defending railroad property. On 1 September, a judge issued a wide-ranging injunction against striking, picketing and other union activity. In the words of one historian, it was 'one of the most extreme pronouncements in American history, violating any number of constitutional guarantees of free speech and free assembly.' Unconstitutional it may have been but it effectively finished off the 1922 railroad strike. It has become known as the 'Daugherty Injunction'.

Daugherty's own political career ended in humiliation. A member of President Harding's 'Ohio Gang' of cronies, he was implicated in the Teapot Dome Scandal (see April) and forced to resign as Attorney General by Harding's successor as president, Calvin Coolidge.

Assassination in London and Berlin

Like so many years of the twentieth century, 1922 was one in which political assassinations made headlines around the world. In London, on 22 June, Sir Henry Wilson was returning from the unveiling of a war memorial at Liverpool Street Station when he was gunned down outside his home in Eaton Place, Belgravia. Some reports, possibly fanciful, suggested that, after the first bullet had been fired, he unsheathed the ceremonial sword he had been wearing to the unveiling and advanced on his attackers, shouting, 'You cowardly swine!' His assassins shot him several more times, killing him, and then fled. Wilson, an Irishman himself, was a former Chief of the Imperial General Staff, the professional head of the British Army, and was hated by many of his fellow countrymen for his role in the Irish War of Independence. The gunmen, both members of the IRA, were Reginald Dunne and Joseph O'Sullivan. As they ran from the scene of the murder, O'Sullivan, who had lost a leg serving in the First World War, was understandably slow and was captured. Dunne, returning to help him, wounded two policemen and a passer-by before he too was taken. Both men were hanged at Wandsworth Prison two months later.

JUNE

Arguably the most significant of all the assassinations of 1922 took place, like that of Sir Henry Wilson, in June. The German Foreign Minister Walther Rathenau was a remarkable man who impressed nearly everyone who knew or met him. According to the writer Stefan Zweig, 'His mind was always on the alert, an instrument of such precision and rapidity as I have never seen in anyone else... He spoke French, English and Italian as well as he did German. His memory never failed him...' He was born in Berlin on 29 September 1867. His father Emil was an astute businessman who had bought the European patents for the electric light bulb Thomas Edison had just invented. Rathenau senior set up a factory which eventually became AEG (Allgemeine Elektrizitäts-Gesellschaft), the biggest German electrical business for the next century, and made him an enormously wealthy man. Walther Rathenau studied the sciences at university, gaining a doctorate in physics, and eventually followed in his father's footsteps. He joined the board of AEG in 1899 and became chairman sixteen years later but he was much more than just a very successful industrialist. He was a man of high culture and great intellect, a visionary who wrote bestselling books on social theory and economics. For a millionaire he had surprising views on capitalism, considering that a system based on the profit motive alone was not likely to be to the long-term benefit of mankind. In 1918, he was one of the founders of the German Democratic Party, a centre-left group that was part of the bubbling melting-pot of politics for most of the years of the Weimar Republic, and his views only moved further to the left in his final years.

In 1921, the German Chancellor, Joseph Wirth,

persuaded Rathenau to join his government as Minister of Reconstruction, a difficult job in the years following the calamity of defeat in the war and in the shadow of the demands made of Germany by the terms of the Treaty of Versailles. Rathenau proved a success in the role but he did not remain in it for long. By the following year Wirth's Foreign Minister, Friedrich Rosen, a long-serving diplomat whose other claim to fame was that he was an expert on Persian poetry, had had enough of the burdens of office. He resigned and Wirth himself acted as his own Foreign Minister for several months but Rathenau was the obvious successor. Initially reluctant, he finally agreed. His mother, who was passionately opposed to him accepting the post at a time of what she saw as such danger, only learned of his acceptance through the newspapers. 'Walther, why have you done this to me?' she asked plaintively when they next met for lunch. 'I really had to, Mama,' he replied, 'because they couldn't find anyone else.'

Frau Rathenau's anxieties soon proved justified. In May, Joseph Wirth received word of a plot to assassinate his recently appointed Foreign Minister. He invited Rathenau to his office to inform him of this and to argue that extra police protection was needed. Rathenau, falling silent, stood still for a long while. According to Wirth, he 'seemed to be gazing on some distant land'. Eventually, Rathenau moved towards Wirth and 'putting both his hands on my shoulders said, "Dear friend, it is nothing. Who would do me any harm?"' As he probably knew in his heart of hearts, he was wrong. There were plenty of people who wished him harm. As a Jew, a millionaire and one of the most prominent members of a government which many Germans hated and considered illegitimate, he was very definitely a potential target for right-wing, anti-Semitic terrorists.

Wirth's informants were correct. There *was* a plot to assassinate Rathenau and it had progressed a long way beyond the kind of boastful rantings in bars and clubs that were commonplace at the time. At its heart were two men in their mid-twenties who had long been involved in the campaigns of the Freikorps, paramilitary groups which had plagued the Weimar Republic since its establishment. Their names were Erwin Kern and Hermann Fischer. Both of them had fought in the war and proved unwilling to accept the consequences of Germany's defeat. Kern had been a lieutenant in the navy; Fischer ended the war as a company commander and had taken part in the so-called Kapp Putsch in 1920, a failed attempt at a right-wing coup in Berlin. Now, together with a motley crew of associates, they plotted to kill the man Kern told a friend 'was greater than all those who surround him' – Rathenau.

The plot came to fruition on the morning of 24 June 1922. At about ten o'clock, the conspirators parked their six-seater car in a side street off the Königsallee in Berlin's Grunewald. They were waiting for Rathenau's open-topped car which they knew always drove slowly along the same route from the foreign minister's house into the centre of the city. When it was spotted, they waited until it passed the end of the side street and then the assassins' car pulled out and followed it. Their vehicle accelerated to overtake and drove slowly past Rathenau's car. An eyewitness, a bricklayer named Krischbin, saw what happened next. Kern 'leaned forward, pulled out a long pistol, rested the butt in his armpit, and opened fire'. A grenade was then thrown and exploded just as Rathenau's chauffeur brought his car to a halt. Surprisingly little damage was done to the vehicle. A nurse named Helene Kaiser, who happened to be passing by, got into the car after the explosion to help the dying man. The politician, she later testified, 'was bleeding hard' but he 'was still alive and was looking up at me'. The chauffeur now drove towards the nearest police station, which was only thirty yards up the street from the scene of the assassination, to inform officers of what had happened. He then returned to Rathenau's house where the injured man was carried into his study. A doctor was called but, by the time he arrived, Rathenau was dead. Five of Kern's bullets had hit him.

Meanwhile, the assassins' car had broken down only a few hundred yards from the scene. They threw their weapons over a garden wall, removed the distinctive leather coats they had been wearing and began to examine their car engine. The police, now in pursuit, sped past them, thinking they were just young men working on their damaged vehicle. Abandoning the car, Kern and his associates then made their way into the centre of the city where news of Rathenau's murder was rapidly percolating. The effects of it were extraordinary. The killing was seen as not just a personal tragedy but a threat to the Weimar regime itself and hundreds of thousands of workers downed tools to rally to its support and condemn the assassins. 'Four deep they marched... beneath their mourning banners,' one observer reported, 'the red of Socialism and the black-red-gold of the Republic, in one endless disciplined procession, passing like a portent silently along the great thoroughfares lined by immense crowds, wave after wave, from the early afternoon till late into the June sunset.' In the Alexanderplatz, in central Berlin, the assassins mingled in the throng and heard angry voices cursing the crime they had just committed.

Clearly, they needed to leave Berlin. They first headed to the Baltic port of Warnemünde where they hoped to find a ship for Sweden but this proved impossible. They had no option but to adopt a less high-tech means of escape and take to bicycles, fleeing southwards through the forests of northern Germany. Within a short while their identities were known. One of the fringe conspirators had decided he valued a financial reward more than he did loyalty to the cause and he had gone to the police. Kern and Fischer were now the most wanted men in Germany. With a price of a million marks on their heads, they eventually took refuge in the deserted Saaleck Castle near Naumburg. They may have hoped to lie low indefinitely but their pictures were now in newspapers and on billboards all over Germany. They were recognised by locals who told police, and detectives were sent to investigate. In the ensuing shoot-out Kern was shot dead by officers, and Fischer turned his gun on himself.

A decade later, the Nazis celebrated and glorified the actions of the assassins. On 17 July 1933, the eleventh anniversary of the deaths of Kern and Fischer, they organised a great parade to their graves where Heinrich Himmler laid a wreath to their memory and Ernst Röhm gave a speech in which he announced that their spirit 'is the spirit of the SS'. (An irony is that many of the conspirators despised the Nazis. One of them, before Hitler came to power, strode up to Goebbels, then Gauleiter of Berlin, and punched him on the side of the head, shouting, 'It wasn't for swine like you that we shot Rathenau!')

There had been other political killings in Weimar Germany. Matthias Erzberger, one of the signatories of the armistice at the end of the First World War, had been shot dead on 26 August 1921 by members of 'Organisation Consul', a right-wing group. Nationalists had also killed Kurt Eisner and Hugo Haase, two socialist politicians, both in 1919. There would be other murders in the years to come. Few of them had the impact of Rathenau's assassination. It had an immediate effect on the stability of the government. Joseph Wirth had again to take on the responsibilities of the Foreign Ministry in addition to his role as Chancellor. By the end of the year he was out of both offices. The killing in the Königsallee also seemed emblematic of the difficulties the Weimar Republic faced in its attempts to establish a democratic state and, with hindsight, a premonition of the hatred, anti-Semitism and political extremism that were to destroy it.

Japanese Withdraw from Siberia

By the beginning of 1922, Japanese soldiers had been fighting in Siberia for four years. They had been part of an international force supporting White Russian troops in their campaigns against the Bolshevik Red Army. This coalition of soldiers from several nations, including Britain, America and Japan, had fallen apart by 1920 and the majority of the troops from other countries had departed. The Japanese stayed on. At one time, they had more than 70,000 soldiers in Siberia. The government had also encouraged major companies, including well-known names like Mitsubishi, to open offices in Vladivostok and other cities, and tens of thousands of Japanese civilians had moved to Siberia. Unlike other nations, Japan had shown a clear desire to remain there and some in the country harboured plans for permanent territorial acquisition but the costs of staying on proved ruinous. The army lost more than 5,000 men through fighting the Russians or through illness and hundreds of millions of yen were spent on the expedition. Increasingly, both political and military leaders in Japan raised their voices calling for withdrawal. On 24 June 1922, the government finally announced that all its troops would leave Siberia by the end of October. Morale amongst those soldiers still stationed there had long been low and there had been incidents in which orders had been disobeyed. Critics of the intervention feared the effects it was having on the army generally.

A new prime minister had taken office only 12 days earlier. Kato Tomosaburo had been Minister of the Navy and Japan's leading delegate to the Washington Naval Conference which had met earlier in the year to discuss international disarmament. He could see little benefit in his country's continued intervention in a foreign country and, despite opposition from some elements in the army, he brought it to an end. With hindsight, the Japanese intervention in Siberia can be seen as a forerunner of its far more serious and destabilising invasion of Manchuria in the 1930s.

July

Future Tarzan Johnny Weissmuller becomes the first man
to swim 100 metres in less than a minute. The British
upper classes adapt to the post-war world and society
weddings such as that of Edwina Ashley and Louis
Mountbatten still hit the headlines. County Hall opens
in London. A book of etiquette is published in the USA
which is still in print today. Jack Dempsey makes his
only defence in the year of his World Heavyweight boxing
title. America's racial divisions continue to engender
hatred and violence, as a lynching in Georgia shows. The
French tennis player Suzanne Lenglen wins the Ladies'
Singles title at Wimbledon for the fourth consecutive year.
The 'Wickedest Man in the World' finishes writing a
novel about drug-taking and sexual excess.

July

Tarzan Breaks a Record

Johnny Weissmuller, two years before winning the first of five Olympic gold medals and a decade before he debuted as probably the most famous Tarzan in movie history, became the first swimmer to post a time of less than a minute for the 100 metres freestyle – only a month past his 18th birthday. Weissmuller had been born in what is now Romania, arriving in the USA with his parents when he was seven months old. He had taken up swimming as a child to combat the effects of polio and soon showed a startling gift for it. The previous year he had become US national champion over both 50 and 220 yards. On 9 July 1922, at Neptune Beach in Alameda, California, Weissmuller recorded a time of 58.6 seconds for 100 metres, easily beating the record held by the Hawaiian-born Duke Kahanamoku. (Kahanamoku was another remarkable athlete, a champion surfer as well as an Olympic gold medal-winning swimmer, who went on to appear in several Hollywood films later in the decade.) Weissmuller made his film debut in 1929, wearing little more than a fig leaf to cover his modesty when he took a cameo role in a musical comedy entitled *Glorifying the American Girl*, but it was his performance as Edgar Rice Burroughs's jungle hero three years later in *Tarzan the Ape Man* which made him a star. He played the character in 11 more films. 'Swimming gave me my start,' Weissmuller later wrote, 'but my pal Tarzan did the real work. He set me up nicely.'

1922

The Mountbattens Marry

The society wedding of the year in Britain took place on 18 July at St Margaret's, Westminster. The king and queen were in attendance. The Prince of Wales was the best man. The bridegroom, a great grandson of Queen Victoria, was Louis Mountbatten. (The name was originally Battenberg but this had been thought too Germanic during the First World War and had been changed.) The bride was a rich heiress named Edwina Ashley. She had some impressive branches on her own family tree, including both the Native American princess Pocahontas and the nineteenth-century Prime Minister Lord Palmerston among her ancestors.

Mountbatten had first heard of his bride-to-be in a letter from a friend who wrote to him about 'a new debutante whom all the young men are mad about... Huge blue eyes, attractive hair, a gorgeous figure and lovely legs; just your cup of tea.' When he met her, in the autumn of 1921, he was smitten. She was equally attracted to the young naval officer. In February 1922, they were both travelling in India. (In retrospect this seems appropriate since, a quarter of a century later, they were to be the last Viceroy and Vicereine of the Raj.) Mountbatten proposed on Valentine's Day and was accepted. When they went their separate ways, now betrothed, he wrote to Edwina, pledging undying love and praising bits of her body he'd been allowed to see, including her breasts which he had dubbed, somewhat unromantically, Mutt and Jeff.

His delight continued after the wedding. 'It's marvellous... being married,' he confided to his mother. Their honeymoon lasted for the rest of the year and took in visits to friends and relatives across Europe. They headed for California where they mingled with Hollywood royalty. At Pickfair, the home owned by Douglas Fairbanks and Mary Pickford, Charlie Chaplin wrote and directed a short film entitled *Nice and Friendly* as a wedding present for the Mountbattens, featuring himself and the couple, together with, as the credits put it, a 'Superior, Startling, Scintillating, Stupendous, Stellar Cast'. Never intended to be anything other than a *jeu d'esprit*, it had no theatrical release but can be seen today, all 11 minutes of it, on YouTube.

However, theirs was not to be a conventional marriage. 'Edwina and I spent all our married lives getting into other people's beds,' Mountbatten later confessed. Her roll-call of lovers is particularly impressive, ranging from minor English aristocrats to the West Indian entertainer Leslie 'Hutch' Hutchinson, a society favourite in the 1930s. Mountbatten himself was slower to break his marital vows but later embarked on a long affair with the wife of a French newspaper tycoon. Despite their serial infidelities, the marriage begun in July 1922 lasted until Edwina's death in 1960.

Opening of County Hall

The day before they attended the Mountbatten wedding George V and Queen Mary performed a more public duty when they formally opened County Hall, the new headquarters of the London County Council on the south bank of the Thames. Following a brief speech by the king, there was a flourish of trumpets and the royal couple were then introduced both to assorted dignitaries and to some of the workmen who had helped to build the vast edifice, still not entirely finished. (Some parts had been disguised so that the royal party would not immediately spot they were incomplete.) After this meet-and-greet session, the king and queen headed for the Council Chamber where Ralph Knott handed George the key with which this room, the heart of its local government function, was officially opened. Knott was County Hall's architect. He was still in his twenties and had only just set up his own practice when he won the commission for the building. Work began on it in 1911 and had been held up during the First World War. It was to continue for many years and Knott was unable to see it finished. He died suddenly and unexpectedly in 1929, aged 50. In 1986, County Hall lost its role as the centre of London government when Margaret Thatcher abolished the LCC. Since then, it has been the site of a variety of businesses including two hotels, the Sea Life London Aquarium and Shrek's Adventure!, a tourist attraction based on animated films about a green ogre.

Emily Post's Etiquette

In the USA, the name of Emily Post remains synonymous with good manners. Her book *Etiquette: in Society, in Business, in Politics and at Home* was first published by Funk & Wagnalls in July 1922. Emily was born into a wealthy Baltimore family and married a prosperous banker when she was in her early twenties. The marriage was not a successful one, largely because of her husband's penchant for messy affairs with chorus girls, and they divorced after 13 years. She turned to writing, producing novels and travel books, but she was over 50 before she found real success with her guide to etiquette. In a swiftly changing American society, where upward mobility was always possible, Emily's instructions on the right ways to behave were greeted with enthusiasm. Immigrants and the newly rich were only too eager to learn from her comprehensive, 620-page volume.

There had been etiquette manuals before but none quite like hers, with its bracing confidence in its own correctness, its breezy style and its cast of fictional characters (the Toploftys, the Richan Vulgars and the Kindharts) used to illustrate Emily's edicts. The original 1922 edition can today often read like despatches from a distant country with very strange and different customs to our own. 'The butler,' Emily announces for the benefit of those who employed such a person, 'never wears the livery of a footman and on no account knee breeches and powder.' She is also certain that, 'it is scarcely an exaggeration to say that those who do not play bridge... are seldom asked out.' She has some surprisingly strict rules about matters which readers now might think pretty unimportant. Which side of a taxi a lady must sit on, for example. 'A lady on the left is *not* a lady,' Emily states unequivocally.

However, there was plenty of more obviously useful advice in her work which struck home for millions who lived in, or, more likely, aspired to live in, polite society. *Etiquette* went through 10 editions and 89 printings before the author's death in 1960. Its 19th edition, edited by her great-great-granddaughter, is still in print today. Emily's career blossomed. She wrote a syndicated column which went out to 160 newspapers, she had her own radio show three times a week and she regularly fielded thousands of letters a week from men and (especially) women seeking her advice.

Jack Dempsey

Only one American sportsman could match the fame of Babe Ruth (see March). In 1922, Jack Dempsey was the World Heavyweight Champion. Nicknamed 'The Manassa Mauler' after the place of his birth in Colorado, he was renowned for the ferocity of his punching and for the relentless aggression with which he fought. Dempsey himself put this down to the toughness of his upbringing and his early experiences of poverty, engaging in impromptu fights in saloons for tiny amounts of cash. 'When I was a young fellow, I was knocked down plenty,' he later said. 'I wanted to stay down, but I couldn't. I had to collect the two dollars for winning or go hungry. I had to get up... You could have hit me on the chin with a sledgehammer for five dollars. When you haven't eaten for two days, you'll understand.' After progressing swiftly up the heavyweight ranks, he had won his title in 1919. His fight against the French boxer Georges Carpentier two years later was the first to generate a million dollars in gate money and the first to be broadcast nationwide on the radio. Dempsey won, knocking out the Frenchman just over a minute into the fourth round. He defended his title only once in

1922 and that was more or less by accident. In July, he was scheduled to appear in an exhibition match in Buffalo, New York, boxing a few rounds against three opponents in quick succession. At the last minute, the New York State Athletic Commission announced that, due to an obscure rule, he could only fight one man, for four rounds, and that his title would be at stake. A light heavyweight named Jimmy Darcy, managed by the same team that managed Dempsey, stepped into the ring with the champion. Darcy, who had been born in Romania as Valeri Trambitas and arrived in the USA when he was nine years old, was a competent fighter but not in the same league as Dempsey. According to a contemporary report, 'The champion took no chances on any adverse decision being given... and boxed in a masterly fashion for the four rounds. At the conclusion the decision was his by a wide margin.' However, had Darcy landed a lucky punch, he would have become a very improbable World Heavyweight Champion. As it was, he could forever boast that he had lasted longer in the ring with Dempsey than both Carpentier and the former heavyweight champion, Jess Willard.

Racial Violence in Georgia

James Harvey and Joe Jordan were African American men, one of them a war veteran, who had spent the early part of 1921 hiking through the Deep South in search of work. In the summer they ended up in Liberty County, Georgia, where they were employed by a local, white farmer. After a few months, they had got into an argument with their white employer over wages they believed he owed them. The employer's wife had then accused them of attacking and raping her. Following a trial in which Harvey and Jordan were denied a proper defence – their court-appointed lawyer made no attempt to collect evidence on their behalf – the two men were sentenced to death. The NAACP (National Association for the Advancement of Colored People) fought their corner, arguing for a retrial, and the date of their execution was several times postponed. Eventually, petitioned by their supporters who had grown in number, Georgia's governor granted the two men a reprieve and reduced their sentence to life imprisonment.

This did not meet with the approval of a section of Liberty County's white population who had already grown tired of the legal delays. On 1 July 1922, a gang of about 50 men seized Harvey and Jordan as they were being transported to jail in Savannah and hanged them by the side of the road. Members of the Savannah NAACP, after ensuring that the lynched men received a decent burial, began to investigate the circumstances in which they had met their deaths. It soon became clear that the deputy sheriff and the law officers whose responsibility it had been to get Harvey and Jordan to prison safely had been complicit in their killing. Witnesses reported to the NAACP investigators that the vehicle in which the two men were being transported had waited for several hours at the roadside until the lynch mob had turned up to haul off their victims. Unusually in a case of lynching, 22 members of the mob, including the deputy sheriff, were indicted for the killings. Four were even convicted, although they received light sentences.

Suzanne Lenglen

On 8 July, the tennis player Suzanne Lenglen won her fourth consecutive Wimbledon Ladies' Singles title. Already a living legend in her native France, where the press dubbed her 'notre Suzanne' and La Divine, Lenglen was perhaps the first female athlete to become a worldwide celebrity. It was not just in France that she hit the headlines. She was news wherever she went. She hobnobbed with royalty and Hollywood stars. Through the distinctive outfits she wore on court, specially created for her by the Paris designer Jean Patou, she became a fashion icon.

In her very first appearance in southwest London in 1919, Lenglen had swept to victory and immediately become a favourite of the Wimbledon faithful. The following year all eyes were upon her. One reporter noted, with heavy irony, that, in the middle of a men's match, 'the crowd, which had seemed happy and contented enough, suddenly surged away in waves that were sucked into Court 4. What was seen there no one who fought his way to the front has apparently survived to tell. Experience, however, connects the seismic disturbance with Mlle Lenglen.' Before long spectators were gathering in their hundreds just to watch her practicing on an outer court in the evening.

Her opponent in her 1922 Wimbledon victory was the Norwegian-American player Molla Mallory, 15 years her senior but still a formidable player (she was to win the last of her 8 US Championship titles in 1926 at the age of 42). However the match lasted only 26 minutes, the shortest singles final in the history of the tournament. Lenglen, at the top of her game, swept Mallory aside, winning 6-2,

6-0. This Wimbledon victory came in the midst of an extraordinary winning streak in which the Frenchwoman went 179 matches without defeat. She went on to win the Wimbledon Singles title for a fifth successive year in 1923 and took it for a sixth time in 1925. Lenglen later became one of the first leading tennis players to relinquish her amateur status and turn professional, thus giving a major boost to the professional game.

She was also one of the first female athletes to market her image successfully. She created a 'Lenglen' brand. Not only did she write a book on tennis (other women players had done this) but she also put her name to a novel. She produced a gramophone record for HMV. In 1934, she appeared in a British musical comedy film entitled *Things Are Looking Up* in which she played the French mistress at a girls' school. (The film also marked the screen debut of Vivien Leigh.) Sadly, her health was beginning to fail her. She died four years later, aged only 39.

Diary of a Drug Fiend

At the end of July Aleister Crowley, while living in Wellington Square, Chelsea, finished dictating the 120,000 words of his novel *Diary of a Drug Fiend* to his 'Scarlet Woman', Leah Hirsig. The book was published by William Collins four months later. Born in Leamington Spa in 1875, Crowley had already enjoyed the 'chequered career' of cliché as a poet, mountaineer, occultist and bohemian but he was now to reach new levels of notoriety. His novel was half-disguised autobiography, clearly based on Crowley's own experiences of drug use, and it was snootily dismissed by an anonymous reviewer in the *Times Literary Supplement* as 'a phantasmagoria of ecstasies, despairs, and above all verbiage'. *The Sunday Express*, however, was outraged. One of its journalists, James Douglas, a man with a reputation for frothing at the mouth when confronted by adventurous literature (he considered Joyce's *Ulysses* 'the apex of lubricity and obscenity'), pulled no punches in his verbal assault on Crowley's work. 'It is a novel describing the orgies of vice practised by a group of moral degenerates,' he wrote and 'at the baser and more bestial horrors of the book,' he went on, 'it is impossible... to hint.' It was, he concluded, 'a book that ought to be burned.' The following weekend, the paper printed a prurient exposé of the author, accusing him of 'preying on the debased' and establishing a hotbed of 'profligacy and vice' at his temple of magic, the Abbey of Thelema on Sicily. (The *Express* had a point. Crowley's activities in Sicily included regular rituals of 'sex magic' and the ingestion of prodigious quantities of cocaine, heroin and other drugs. It was all a long way from the kind of suburban pleasures preferred by the average *Sunday Express* reader.)

The Express's lambasting of his life and work had an ambivalent effect on Crowley's fortunes. On the one hand, it showed that, even in 1922, no publicity was bad publicity. The first edition of *Diary of a Drug Fiend* sold out before the end of the year. On the other, Crowley's publisher, William Collins, was appalled by the furore. He refused to print a second edition and cancelled a contract Crowley had signed to write an autobiography.

Crowley's troubles only mounted in the following

year. Led by the *Express* and other newspapers owned by Lord Beaverbrook, the press continued to hound him. One magazine dubbed him 'The Wickedest Man in the World' and the title was to follow him for the rest of his life. As rumours about the unholy goings-on at his 'Abbey' continued to flourish, Mussolini's government insisted that he and his followers leave Italy. He was obliged to re-embark on his peripatetic life as an occultist and practitioner of 'Magick'.

August

Alexander Graham Bell's death is suitably
commemorated throughout the USA. In China a
typhoon causes thousands of deaths in the coastal city of
Swatow. The assassination of Michael Collins in Ireland
is a significant moment in the country's civil war. The
Jazz Age is in full swing and Louis Armstrong's journey
from New Orleans to Chicago marks a turning point in
the music's history. Also in Chicago, a young gangster gets
his first taste of notoriety. The Ku Klux Klan spreads its
tentacles across America as a trial in California reveals
some of its inherent absurdities. Britain's greatest press
baron dies and, in London, a hero seeks to escape the
fame his First World War exploits brought him.

Telephones Fall Silent

At 6.30 pm Eastern Standard Time on 4 August, every single one of the 13 million telephones in the USA went out of action for a minute. The reason was neither a nationwide malfunction nor a strike of telephone operators. It was a deliberate withdrawal of the service as a mark of respect to the man who had made the first phone call, summoning his assistant from another room ('Mr Watson, come here, I want to see you'), 46 years earlier. The Scottish-born inventor Alexander Graham Bell had died at his home in Nova Scotia on 2 August and the silencing of all American phones was timed to coincide with his funeral. Ironically, Bell had lost much of his interest in his most famous invention many years before his death. As obituaries reported, he had told reporters on his 75th birthday in March that he would not have a telephone in his own study and his daughter-in-law's home in Miami, where he had spent his last winter working on other inventions, did not have one.

Although he is today remembered chiefly for the invention of the telephone, Bell was also a remarkable man in many other ways. When he and his family emigrated to Canada in 1870, they took up residence close to a large First Nations reserve in Ontario. Bell became fascinated by the Mohawk language and translated its unwritten vocabulary into Visible Speech, a system of phonetic symbols for helping the deaf to speak which his father had devised. The younger Bell was made an honorary chief of the Mohawk and was initiated into some of their ceremonies, including traditional dances. In later life, he was likely, during moments of excitement, to break into a Mohawk war dance.

His other inventions and patents included ones for an early metal detector, a type of phonograph, several for 'hydroairplanes' and something he called a 'photophone' which was intended to transmit speech via a beam of light. He thought it his 'greatest invention' and 'greater than the telephone'. At one point he even wanted to make 'Photophone' his second daughter's middle name but was persuaded by his wife that this was not a good idea. Despite Bell's enthusiasm, the photophone never took off.

His lifelong interest in helping the deaf had its origins in his father's work and in his own mother's deafness which had deeply affected him when he was a boy growing up in Edinburgh. As a young man he worked as a teacher for the deaf and first met with the remarkable Helen Keller who overcame the loss of both her sight and hearing as a very small child to become a world-renowned author, lecturer and pioneering advocate of disability rights. In the 1880s and 1890s, using money he had gained from his inventions, he established first the Volta Laboratory and then the Volta Bureau which were dedicated to studying deafness and improving the life of the deaf. On the announcement of his death, Felix H Levey, president of the American Institution for the Improved Instruction of Deaf Mutes, stated that, 'Entirely apart from the monumental achievement of Professor Bell as the inventor of the telephone, his conspicuous work in [sic] behalf of the deaf of this country would alone entitle him to everlasting fame.'

AUGUST

The Swatow Typhoon

The conditions for a developing typhoon had first been spotted in the Pacific Ocean on 27 July. It gathered force as it crossed over the northernmost extremes of the Philippines, entered the South China Sea and made landfall on the Chinese coast near Swatow on the night of 2-3 August. It was accompanied by an enormous tidal wave which swept across mud flats into the streets of the coastal city. Now known as Shantou, and with a population of more than 5 million, Swatow was then one of the treaty ports opened in the nineteenth century to trade with the west. The winds which hit the coast around the port were ferocious, blowing at over 100 mph. Ships were found which had been carried more than two miles inland by the typhoon.

Many of Swatow's inhabitants lived not in permanent dwellings but on sampans and other craft moored along the nearby coastline which made them particularly vulnerable. Of the 65,000 people who called the city home, more than 50,000 are thought to have died in the typhoon and the loss of life in the surrounding region was considerable. It is estimated that the total death toll may have been as high as 100,000. A meteorologist at the time stated that, 'This will go down in history as one of the worst, if not the worst typhoon, that has ever visited the Far East.'

Contemporary newspaper reports in Australia and the USA compared the devastation to that of the First World War. 'The scenes resemble those at Ypres during the war,' one claimed. 'The storm has destroyed all stocks of food and water supplies... Swatow is now under 10 feet of water.

The harbour is full of floating dead bodies, and famine is raging.' The widespread destruction severely hampered rescue efforts. Corpses which had been gathered together had to lie unburied because there were no coffins in which to put them. All the piers and pontoons in the harbour had been broken into matchwood, making it impossible to land relief supplies. It took many years for the city to recover.

The Killing of Michael Collins

August was not a good month for those on the pro-Treaty side in the ongoing Irish Civil War. On its very first day, their most charismatic leader, Michael Collins, was reminded of the terrible divisions the war was creating when Harry Boland died in St Vincent's Hospital, Dublin. A close friend of Collins, Boland had opposed the Treaty and thus placed himself on the other side of the great chasm which had opened up in Ireland. He had been shot several days earlier by soldiers from the Free State Army who had come to arrest him. Collins was moved by the death of his old comrade in the struggle to end British rule. 'I passed Vincent's Hospital and saw a small crowd outside,' he wrote. 'My mind went into him lying dead there and I thought of the times together... I'd send a wreath but I suppose they'd return it torn up.'

On 12 August, Arthur Griffith died suddenly. Griffith, co-signer of the Treaty with Collins, had collapsed unconscious while bending down to tie a loose shoelace. Doctors were on hand when he recovered consciousness but they were unable to help. He fell again, blood pouring from his mouth and he died as a priest administered extreme unction. He was 51 years old. The official cause of death was a cerebral haemorrhage but few doubted that it had been brought on by overwork and stress.

Griffith's death was a terrible blow but the worst was yet to come. Collins himself was to fall victim to the civil war before the month was over. There had been previous attempts to kill him. In April, shots had been fired when he and a group of friends alighted from a taxi outside a Dublin hotel. On 11 August, Collins, together with an escort of troops, set out on what was intended to be an inspection tour of the national army's South Western Command. News of Griffith's death brought him back to Dublin for the funeral but he then set off once more for Cork where he stayed two nights at the Imperial Hotel which had been taken over by the army.

Just after 6 on the morning of 22 August, Collins, together with his trusted comrade Emmet Dalton and a small convoy of motor cycles and cars, one of them armoured, left the Imperial. They were planning to travel through some of the most aggressively anti-Treaty areas of the county and, an hour or so outside Cork, they halted briefly in the tiny village of Béal na mBláth. Collins seemed to have shaken off the depression and ill-health from which he had been noticeably suffering in recent weeks. When he stopped later at the pub owned by his cousin Jeremiah, he was in bullish mood. 'I'm going to settle this thing,' he was heard to say. 'I'm going to put an end to this bloody war.' His presence in the middle of what was largely hostile, anti-Treaty territory had, of course, been noticed and plans had been made to ambush his convoy at Béal na mBláth if it returned to Cork by the same route. Common sense might have dictated that Collins and those with him should travel back by different roads and it is not clear why they did not. Perhaps there were few alternatives. Many of the local roads had been blocked off and bridges had been blown up.

For whatever reason, the convoy approached Béal na mBláth for the second time that day at around 7.30 pm. Many of the anti-Treaty IRA men, who had been hanging around the village most of the day, had left, assuming that Collins had indeed chosen another route back, but a handful were still there, waiting in ambush, and they began to fire. Emmet Dalton ordered the driver to 'drive like hell' but Collins countermanded this instruction, shouting out, 'Stop! We'll fight them.' After shooting back at the attackers from behind the armoured car, Collins saw that some of them were moving position and ran about fifteen yards up the road before dropping to the ground and continuing to fire his gun. According to Dalton, it was soon after this that he heard a faint cry of 'Emmet, I'm hit'. When he moved in its direction, he found Collins lying face down in the road. He had a gaping head wound and, although he was conscious when Dalton reached him, it was clear that he was dying. 'Very gently I raised his head on my knee,' Dalton later wrote, 'and tried to bandage his wound but owing to the awful size of it this proved very difficult. I had not completed this task when the big eyes quickly closed, and the cold pallor of death overspread the General's face.'

Immediately after signing the Anglo-Irish Treaty in

December 1921, Collins had written gloomily to a friend that, 'I have signed my death warrant.' His words had proved prophetic. His body was carried back to Cork and then transported by sea to the Irish capital. The funeral was held on 28 August. Collins's coffin was borne in procession on a gun carriage through the streets of Dublin before he was interred in the city's Glasnevin Cemetery. A month after the assassination, much of the major fighting had ceased, although outbreaks of violence continued in parts of the country throughout the rest of the year and the first months of the next. The Irish Civil War officially came to an end in May 1923, when the IRA announced a ceasefire, but its legacy cast a shadow over Irish politics for the rest of the twentieth century. In 1948, the judge and politician Kingsmill Moore wrote, 'Even now Irish politics is largely dominated by the bitterness of the hunters and the hunted of 1922.' His words continued to resonate for decades to come. Today, the two main political parties in Ireland are still Fine Gael and Fianna Fáil. Both have their roots in the conflict a century ago.

All That Jazz

If the decade isn't described as 'The Roaring Twenties', more often than not it's called 'The Jazz Age'. The term is usually said to have been invented by F Scott Fitzgerald. Although a few others had used it before, it was certainly Fitzgerald who brought it to wider public attention with *Tales of the Jazz Age*, the title of his volume of short stories, first published in 1922. Jazz, particularly in America, was the background music to many of the defining events of the 1920s. There were those who were unconverted to its delights. Doctors warned of its dangers. Did jazz 'put the sin into syncopation', as one magazine article put it? Some people certainly thought so. The *Ladies' Home Journal* launched an anti-jazz crusade, its editors thrown into a tizzy by the immorality it supposedly encouraged and the dancing, characterised by 'wriggling movement and sensuous stimulation', which accompanied it. They urged its 'legal prohibition'. Meanwhile, the author and diplomat Henry van Dyke called jazz, 'an unmitigated cacophony, a species of music invented by demons for the torture of imbeciles'. But the *Ladies' Home Journal* could hardly claim to have its finger on the pulse of the *zeitgeist* and van Dyke had been born in 1852. Jazz was not intended for middle-class matrons and septuagenarians. It was the music of the younger, post-war generation and they lapped it up. Some of the greatest names in the history of jazz – Kid Ory, Sidney Bechet, Coleman Hawkins, Fats Waller – were already playing. Duke Ellington and Count Basie were embarking on their careers. A watered-down version of African American jazz was being purveyed to white audiences by white bandleaders like Paul Whiteman who were often more famous than their black counterparts. (Whiteman had the gall to claim that his jazz would 'remove the stigma of barbaric strains and jungle cacophony' from the music.) However, the year's most significant jazz event would have passed unnoticed by most people.

The cultural critic Kevin Jackson has called 8 August 1922 'possibly the single most important day in the history of jazz'. It was on that date that the 21-year-old New Orleans cornet player, Louis Armstrong, already a well-known musician in Louisiana and on the Mississippi riverboats, took a train from his native city to Chicago. He had been invited to join King Oliver and his Creole Jazz Band. 'I arrived in Chicago about eleven o'clock at night,' he later wrote, '... I was all eyes looking out the window when the train pulled into the station. Anyone watching me closely could have easily seen that I was a country boy.'

Playing with King Oliver, Armstrong soon began to feel more at home and he was astonished by the quality of the music he was hearing in the city's clubs and bars. He had always assumed that New Orleans was the jazz capital of the USA but now he had to rethink his ideas. 'I was scared to go eat because I might miss one of those good notes,' he confessed.

August also saw the Broadway premiere of a 'jazz' opera by George Gershwin. This was not the much more famous *Porgy and Bess*, which dates from the 1930s, but *Blue Monday* which was staged as part of the revue *George White's Scandals of 1922* on 28 August. Gershwin, approaching his 24th birthday, had worked before for the impresario George White and was commissioned to produce a piece which might rival the success of *Shuffle Along*, a hit from the previous year with black performers. Working with the lyricist Buddy DeSylva, he produced *Blue Monday*. All the roles in this one-act tale of a gambler shot dead by his jealous lover, are African American characters but, in a casting decision that seems almost unbelievable a hundred years later, they were played by white singers in blackface. It was not a success. The audience for a Broadway revue was not prepared for a doomed Harlem love affair. White, realising that *Blue Monday* was not quite what his show required, dropped it after the first night. Re-orchestrated and renamed *135th Street*, the piece had a concert performance at Carnegie Hall a few years later but its real importance lies in the fact that, as an example of what was sometimes called 'symphonic jazz', it paved the way for Gershwin's later works such as *Rhapsody in Blue* and *Porgy and Bess*.

The Inglewood Raid

During the 1920s, the Ku Klux Klan was expanding its membership and influence throughout the United States (see November). Although it was strongest in the Deep South, it even had support in California where its activities were brought to wider public notice by the trial of 37 of its members in Inglewood, a city in Los Angeles County. They faced court on 7 August 1922 for events which had happened several months earlier.

The plan had been for the Klan to attack the family home of Fidel Elduayen, reportedly a bootlegger who had sold bad liquor which had killed one man and blinded another. The raid didn't get off to a good start when it was discovered that there were not enough white robes to go around. Participants were told to create masks from their handkerchiefs. With these improvised coverings in place, the group descended on the Elduayen household where they tied up Fidel and his brother Mathias and threatened to kill them. Disturbed by the noise and by the sight of swarms of men next door with handkerchiefs tied around their faces, Elduayen's neighbour phoned the local constable, Medford B Mosher. He didn't answer. He couldn't because he was one of the Klansmen paying the Elduayens an unannounced visit. The neighbour then tried the City Marshal's office and had better luck. Two officers arrived on the scene on a motorbike to be greeted by Klansmen waving guns in the air. There was a short exchange of shots and one of the Klansmen fell to the ground, fatally wounded. It was Medford B Mosher. Two other Klansmen were shot, although they recovered from their injuries. Both of them were also law officers.

A coroner's inquest was held on the Monday following the raid. Evidence was taken from all sides, including from the local Klan's Grand Goblin (the Klan had a taste for ludicrous titles as well as words beginning with 'K'), a man named William Coburn. He claimed that there could not have been any Klansmen among the mob at the Elduayen house. He had been there and he'd walked around, giving his 'Grand Goblin's call' and nobody responded. Unsurprisingly, the coroner and later the grand jury failed to find his testimony conclusive and, at the beginning of June, Coburn and 36 others were indicted on charges of false imprisonment, kidnapping and assault. The trial opened on 7 August and there was soon drama when one of the Klan leaders 'crumpled up with a convulsion' while listening to one of the Elduayen children give evidence and had to be carried from the courtroom. The prosecution sought to show that the raid had been entirely unlawful from the beginning; the defence argued that it was a justifiable response to the illegal selling of liquor. The jury agreed with the defence and the Klansmen were all acquitted. Immediately after the verdict Fidel and Mathias Elduayen were themselves arrested and charged with offences against the Volstead Act, which had established Prohibition in America three years earlier. The case against them dragged on until February 1924 when the two brothers were finally acquitted.

Death of a Press Baron

Alfred Harmsworth, 1st Viscount Northcliffe, died on 14 August, aged 57. According to a rival newspaper owner, Lord Beaverbrook, Northcliffe was 'the greatest figure who ever strode down Fleet Street'. He had certainly done more than any other contemporary to shape the British press. Born near Dublin in 1865, Harmsworth began his career as a journalist but soon decided that owning papers and magazines was a better route to fortune than writing for them. In partnership with his brother, he started the weekly *Answers to Correspondents* when he was in his early twenties. In the 1890s, he bought the failing *Evening News* and through what were then innovative techniques (eye-catching headlines, imaginative use of illustrations), turned it into a success. He founded the *Daily Mail*, still published today from Northcliffe House in Kensington, in 1896. Although snootily dismissed by the Prime Minister, Lord Salisbury, as 'by office boys for office boys', the *Mail* rapidly became a bestselling paper and Harmsworth added to his burgeoning empire by creating the *Daily Mirror* in 1903. Five years later he entered the heart of the Establishment when he bought *The Times*. In parallel with his newspaper career, Harmsworth also created the Amalgamated Press which was, at one time, the largest publisher in the world, and produced a range of periodicals from *Comic Cuts* (slogan: 'Amusing Without Being Vulgar') to *Film Fun* and school story magazines such as *The Magnet*, home of Billy Bunter. Cheaply priced, Harmsworth's productions put an end to one strand of Victorian publishing. In AA Milne's words, he 'killed the penny dreadful by the simple process of producing the ha'penny dreadfuller.' In his last years, Northcliffe was plagued by ill health, both physical, probably as a result of relentless overwork, and mental, which some have claimed was the result of syphilis. He grew increasingly paranoid and delusional, believing that people were out to kill him. On one occasion he told the editor of *The Times* that the sound of a blind cord hitting a window was actually that of someone taking a potshot at him. He spent his final days looked after by private nurses, alternately promising them rich rewards for their services or threatening them with violence if they didn't do what he wanted.

Lawrence of Arabia Joins the RAF

On 30 August 1922, a man who gave his name as John Hume Ross turned up at the RAF recruiting office in Henrietta Street in London's Covent Garden. He failed the medical examination and, when asked, he could produce no birth certificate. The recruiting officer was unimpressed by the prospective recruit who was, the officer later wrote, 'a thin pale-faced chap' and 'there was something so off-hand about his manner, almost amounting to insolence, that I took an instant dislike to him.' He was all for rejecting him. He was prevented from doing so. Despite all the reasons for showing John Ross the door, the officer in Henrietta Street was sent instructions that the man should be allowed to enlist. John Hume Ross had friends in high places.

He was, in reality, TE Lawrence, known to nearly everyone in the country as Lawrence of Arabia. In the years since his exploits in the First World War, when he had joined forces with Arab rebels to fight against the armies of Germany's ally, the Ottoman Empire, Lawrence had become adept at what one friend called 'backing into the limelight'. He both yearned for attention and claimed to despise it. By 1922, his fame had become all too much for him and he craved anonymity. He decided that this would best be achieved if he joined the RAF as a humble aircraftman and he was more than prepared to pull strings to ensure that this was possible. The recruiting officer in Covent Garden, who complained to his superiors about the appalling irregularity of the procedure, and was told, 'Watch your step, this man is Lawrence of Arabia, get him in or you'll get your bowler hat' (in other words, his marching orders), later went on to his own form of fame. His name was WE Johns and he was to become the creator of Biggles, the pilot hero of dozens of boys' adventures published from the 1930s to the 1960s.

Aircraftman Second Class John Ross was posted to an air training depot in Uxbridge. Later in the year he was sent to the school of photography at RAF Farnborough. For a brief while he proved a model student. 'Nothing about him,' one of the officers at Farnborough later remembered, 'suggested that here was the most amazing aircraftman ever to join the RAF.' But his cover was about to be blown. The press was on to him. On 27 December 1922, the *Daily Express* reported, wrongly, that he had joined the army as a private. Other newspapers learned the truth and, for two weeks, Farnborough became the centre of a media feeding frenzy. Reporters could not believe that Lawrence would simply hide away, and speculated that there was some secret motive for his actions. 'There is something that this indefatigable searcher after knowledge knew the RAF could teach him,' the *News of the World* confidently asserted, 'or somewhere it was going he desired to go also.' The publicity forced Lawrence out of the RAF and he joined the army under the name of Shaw. He hated it and petitioned his friends in the RAF to reinstate him. This was finally arranged in 1925 and Lawrence of Arabia gained yet another identity as Aircraftman TE Shaw. Ten years later, soon after his departure from the RAF for a second time (his period of enlistment had come to an end), Lawrence/Shaw was involved in an accident on his motorbike and was thrown over its handlebars. He suffered serious injuries and died six days later.

Al Capone Arrested

Early in the morning of 30 August, 23-year-old Alphonse 'Al' Capone was driving at speed along North Wabash Avenue in Chicago. He had been drinking and lost control of his car which crashed into a parked taxi cab. Undamaged,

Capone hauled himself from his wrecked vehicle, waving a revolver in the air, and threatened to shoot the taxi driver Fred Krause. In his intoxicated state Capone may have thought Krause was a rival racketeer attempting to kill him, although the cabbie had just been sitting peaceably in his car when it had been hit. Still enraged, Capone also pointed his weapon at shocked bystanders. The conductor of a passing trolley car bravely advised him to put his gun back in his pocket and was told, in no uncertain terms, that he should shut up and move on. Police soon arrived and, although Capone was now waving a deputy sheriff's badge which had somehow come into his possession and which, he claimed, gave him immunity from the law, they arrested him. Krause, who had been injured in the collision, was taken off in an ambulance.

Making his first appearance in the Chicago papers as 'Alfred Caponi', the junior gangster was described as living at 'the notorious Four Deuces, a disorderly house at 2222 South Wabash Avenue'. Initially charged with assault with an automobile, driving while intoxicated and carrying a concealed weapon, he was not brought to trial. His boss, the mobster Johnny Torrio, pulled strings to make sure he went free. Despite his youth, Capone was already a feared member of the city's organised crime gangs. Born in New York, he had joined the Five Points Gang in the city as a teenager, but moved to Chicago at the age of 20 at Torrio's suggestion. He became Johnny Torrio's enforcer and protégé, and eventually inherited his crime empire when the older man decided the gangster life was too dangerous and left for Italy. Supposedly, Torrio handed over power with the words, 'It's all yours, Al. Me? I'm quitting. It's

Europe for me.' Capone, still only 26, was launched on his career as America's most famous racketeer and the man behind the infamous St Valentine's Day Massacre of 1929. Famously, despite several other arrests, he was only finally convicted in 1931, and sent to prison, for tax evasion. Released in 1939 because of his failing health, he suffered from syphilis which he had probably contracted while working as the bouncer at a brothel when he first arrived in Chicago. He died in Florida in 1947.

September

A fire destroys one of the finest cities of the old Ottoman
Empire amidst scenes of bloody violence and appalling
loss of life. In America, a pilot crosses the country
from Atlantic to Pacific for the first time and a double
murder in New Jersey hits the headlines. The staging of
a play by a debut dramatist in Munich marks the start
of one of the twentieth century's most influential theatre
careers. A women's football team from Lancashire draws
the crowds during its tour of America. Riots in New
York erupt over whether or not to wear a particular type
of headgear. A French-Senegalese war hero becomes a
boxing world champion.

The Great Fire of Smyrna

Smyrna in the summer of 1922 was one of the world's most cosmopolitan cities. 'In no city... did East and West mingle physically in so spectacular a fashion,' wrote George Horton, the American consul there. It was situated in Turkey but it was dominated by its Greek population which numbered some 320,000. And yet all kinds of nationalities made their homes in Smyrna. 'You saw all sorts...' a French journalist later recalled. 'Swiss hoteliers, German traders, Austrian tailors, English mill owners, Dutch fig merchants, Italian brokers, Hungarian bureaucrats, Armenian agents and Greek bankers.' It was a great commercial entrepôt and, even after the horrors and upheavals of the war years (which had touched it less than other parts of the dying Ottoman Empire), it remained a city of great prosperity, sophistication and charm. Despite this, it was in Smyrna, in two weeks of September 1922, that one of the great human tragedies of the twentieth century unfolded.

The appalling events in Smyrna were the unplanned consequences of the chaos that followed the war and the conflict between two visions of the future of Anatolia. On the one hand there was the ambition of Kemal Atatürk (as he later became known) to replace the splintering Ottoman Empire with a new, modernising and united Turkish nation; on the other there was the dream of the Greek politician Eleftherios Venizelos – the so-called 'Megali Idea' ('Great Idea') – of expanding the Greek state to include all those areas of Anatolia which had a significant Greek population. The two projects were clearly incompatible and confrontation between Greeks and Turks was inevitable.

With the backing of allies such as the British Prime Minister David Lloyd George, Greek forces landed at Smyrna in May 1919, taking control of the city and its environs. The following year saw a succession of Greek advances ever further into the Anatolian hinterland. By the summer of 1921, the Greeks were in the ascendant and the Turkish nationalists, under the ultimate command of Kemal, were in retreat. The Greek king, Constantine I, had had a chequered career as monarch, including a period in exile when he was replaced by his son Alexander. Alexander died at the age of 27, after being bitten by a pet monkey and developing fatal sepsis, and his father was restored to the throne. Now Constantine made a triumphant visit to Smyrna, where he was given a hero's welcome by the city's Greek inhabitants. Constantine was unimpressed by what he saw of Turkey and firmly believed that further Greek expansion was required. The Turks were incapable of progress and, he wrote, 'it is high time they disappeared once more and went back into the interior of Asia, whence they came.' Plenty of his troops and generals agreed with him. They were more than prepared to drive the Turks back but they underestimated both their opponents and the terrain they faced.

By the beginning of September 1921, Greek troops were in the heartland of Turkey but their offensive was grinding to a halt. Worse than that, their supply lines were stretched to breaking point and under constant attack by Turkish irregulars. Eventually, they were forced to retreat and take shelter. The Greek army was now stranded in the middle of Anatolia, unable to go forward or back. The only option for them was to dig in and hope for the best.

For the best part of 12 months, the once triumphant but now increasingly demoralised Greek soldiers were trapped in their precarious positions in central Anatolia. Their prospects were not made brighter by the man who had somehow found himself in overall command of the so-called Army of Asia Minor. General Georgios Hatzianestis had already had a chequered military career. By the late summer of 1922, he had developed serious mental health problems. On some days, he suffered from the delusion that his feet were made of glass and he refused to stand up for fear of breaking them. Unsurprisingly, many observers thought he was better suited to incarceration in a lunatic asylum than to his role as commander-in-chief of an army.

The troops under his command were in a poor state – weary, far from home and utterly demoralised. On 26 August Kemal gave his soldiers orders to attack. 'Your goal is the Mediterranean,' he told them. Within days, the Turkish troops were entirely victorious. Battalions of Greek soldiers were wiped out, almost to a man. Tens of thousands of prisoners were taken. Fleeing the field in disarray, the survivors headed for the coast as best they could, pausing only to torch the towns and villages they passed through. Soon vast numbers of individuals, both military and civilian, were on the move, trying to escape the chaos. By 6 September the first of these fugitives from the turmoil inland were arriving in the outskirts of Smyrna. One witness wrote in a letter of 'endless streams of disbanded Greek soldiers'. They were, she went on, 'A miserable rabble, ragged, weary and wan; and with them were hundreds of refugees, both Greek and Turkish, plodding their way under a burning sun, through clouds of hot dust swirling in the air.'

As the next day dawned, there were more than 100,000 of these destitute refugees camped out in the streets of Smyrna and thousands more were being added every hour. When Kemal's pursuing troops first entered the city in triumph on Saturday 9 September, they appeared to be highly disciplined. Gloomy predictions about the chaos and destruction they would bring seemed misplaced. Hortense Wood, a member of one of the prosperous commercial dynasties who formed the top rank in Smyrniot society, noted in her diary, 'Perfect discipline and perfect quiet. Not a shot was fired. And thus came the change from Greek to Turkish administration, in perfect tranquillity and against all expectations and apprehensions.' Extra reassurance for Smyrna's citizens came from the presence in the harbour of battleships belonging to Europe's great powers, including eleven from Britain and five from France. Surely they would protect the city from anything the Turkish troops might inflict upon it?

However, there were still plenty among the Greek and Armenian communities who were terrified by the arrival of Kemal's men. And it was they, rather than optimists such as Hortense Wood, who were to prove correct. By the Sunday morning, Turkish soldiers had embarked on a rampage through Smyrna's Armenian quarter. Some were irregulars, and were not part of Kemal's army, but others undoubtedly were. Metropolitan Chrysostom, the Greek Orthodox Church's senior cleric in Smyrna, emerging from a meeting with the Turkish commander-in-chief, was confronted by an angry mob. He was seized by the crowd and subjected to the most appalling torments. According to an eyewitness, 'They began to beat him with their fists and sticks and to spit on his face. They riddled him with stabs. They tore his beard off, they gouged his eyes out, they cut off his nose and ears.' French soldiers, wishing to intervene, were prevented from doing so by their commanding officer, who was under strict orders to remain neutral. The mutilated Metropolitan was dragged into a backstreet where he died of his wounds. Seventy years later, he was declared a martyr and a saint of his Church.

The situation in Smyrna continued to deteriorate. By the Tuesday morning the city was heaving with the tens of thousands of refugees, nearly all of them Greeks fleeing from the fighting inland, and more were continuing to arrive every hour. They were increasingly at the mercy of Turkish soldiers whose discipline had now broken down almost completely. Officers proved to have little authority over their men. Greeks and Armenians in Smyrna became the targets of brutal assaults and atrocities. The city was rapidly descending into a state of anarchy. Looting, murder and rape were commonplace. The Reverend Charles Dobson, vicar of the Anglican church in Smyrna, was an appalled witness to the horrors. When he bravely ventured out into the city, he saw corpses lying everywhere. 'There was constantly shooting in the back streets,' he wrote, 'followed by screams and panic-stricken running. The Turks were openly looting everywhere.' Perhaps the most terrible scenes he encountered were in the Armenian quarter. 'I was particularly struck with one group [of bodies] consisting of women and babies; and a young girl, almost nude, shot through the breast and with clotted blood on her thighs and genital organs that spoke only too clearly of her fate before death.'

Dobson may have thought that no worse disaster could strike the city but he would have been wrong. The following day, fire took hold of the Greek and Armenian areas of Smyrna. Controversy still rages over who was responsible for starting it but most of the evidence points to Turkish soldiers deliberately setting fire to buildings. On Monday an Armenian priest had seen 'the Turks taking bombs, gunpowder, kerosene and everything necessary to start fires, in wagonfuls here and there through the streets.' By dusk on the Wednesday the quayside was packed with what some have estimated as nearly half a million people, driven to the waterfront by the wall of fire. 'The screams of the frantic mob on the quay could easily be heard a mile distant,' one observer noted. 'There was a choice of three kinds of death: the fire behind, the Turks waiting at the side streets and the ocean in front.'

The Anglican clergyman, Charles Dobson, who had shepherded large groups of British nationals to the safety of battleships in the bay, looked back on the city in dismay. It was, 'One appalling mass of flames, the waterfront covered with dark masses of despairing humanity.' By Friday morning, the sea was full of floating corpses. Grotesquely, dozens of young Turkish men and boys were swimming amongst them, looking for items of value to steal. 'Their noses were covered by scarves tied on the back of their heads, so they wouldn't breathe in the stench of rotting bodies,' one observer noted. 'They held a sharp knife and skilfully cut from the bodies the fingers that wore rings, and the ends of the ears that wore earrings, to take those jewels.' It is little wonder that one of those lucky enough to escape the city later wrote, 'One of the keenest impressions which I brought away with me from Smyrna was a feeling of shame that I belonged to the human race.'

Jimmy Doolittle Crosses America

On 4-5 September, Jimmy Doolittle, later to become famous for the World War Two 'Doolittle Raid' on Tokyo, made the first single-day crossing of the United States from the Atlantic to the Pacific. In 21 hours and 19 minutes, he flew from Jacksonville, Florida to San Diego, California with only one hour-long stop for refuelling in Texas. Soon after landing, Doolittle gave newspaper reporters his own account of the flight. He had hit bad weather a couple of hours after take-off, flying into a heavy thunderstorm. 'It was pitch black,' he told journalists, 'but I had no trouble picking out landmarks by the frequent flashes of lightning.' The rain had accompanied him all the way to San Antonio, Texas but Doolittle, as was the habit of laconic heroes of the time, made light of the dangers he had faced. 'Did you have any trouble?' he was asked. 'Not a bit of any kind,' he replied. The most to which he would admit was a slight feeling of hunger after his trip. 'I could eat a little,' he told well-wishers after he brought his de Havilland DH 4 into land at Rockwell Field, San Diego.

1922

The Hall-Mills Murders

If the headline-grabbing murder trial in Britain in 1922 was that of Edith Thompson and Freddy Bywaters (see December) then the American equivalent was probably the Hall-Mills case. On 6 September, teenage factory worker Pearl Bahmer and her older beau, Raymond Schneider, were out for a walk in countryside near the town of New Brunswick, New Jersey. Venturing down a little-used path, they were surprised to see two people lying beneath a crab apple tree. Pearl walked slowly towards them and then called out to her companion. 'Come here! These people ain't breathin'!' She and her boyfriend had stumbled across the dead bodies of clergyman Edward Wheeler Hall and his lover, choir member Eleanor Mills. Both had been shot through the head, Hall once and Mills three times. In addition, the woman's throat had been cut. In a grisly detail, it was noted that, because the bodies had been lying there for at least a day and a half, the wound in Mills's neck 'was entirely filled with maggots'.

The victims were well known in New Brunswick. Reverend Hall was the pastor of the Episcopal Church of St John the Evangelist in the town and Mrs Mills sang in the church's choir. As many local people knew, or at least suspected, the pair had been lovers. 'The rector can't find time to call on me once a year but he manages to call on Mrs Mills eight or nine times a week,' one parishioner bitchily remarked. Any doubts about their relationship were dispelled by the contents of the love letters which were found torn into pieces and scattered in the grass around the corpses. 'I want to look up into your dear face for hours as you touch my body close,' Eleanor Mills had written. The pastor had been just as passionate in reply. 'I want to see you Friday night alone by our road,' he told her, 'where we can let out, unrestrained, that universe of joy and happiness we call ours.' He signed himself DTL or, in German, 'Dein Treuer Liebhaber' ('Your True Lover'); she referred to him, more colloquially, as 'Babykins'.

Unsurprisingly, the murders, with their tantalising mix of sex, violence and religion in a seemingly respectable setting, attracted nationwide attention. Tabloid newspapers grew ever more frenzied in their coverage. Ghoulish tourists by the hundreds arrived in the lane where the bodies were found. They stripped off the bark on the crab apple tree, under which the Reverend Hall and Mrs Mills had been carefully placed, seeking souvenirs. Vendors selling popcorn and soft drinks pitched up at the site.

Although Mrs Hall and her two brothers were suspected of carrying out the killings, no indictments followed the first investigation. It was not until four years had passed that the state governor, under pressure from newspaper stories about new evidence, ordered a second investigation. In November 1926, Mrs Hall and her brothers were finally brought to trial but they were acquitted. Over the decades since then, various theories about the killings have been put forward, some more plausible than others. One writer even suggested that the pair were killed by members of the Ku Klux Klan, outraged by Hall and Mills flouting the rules of what the Klan saw as moral decency. The case remains unsolved, although most of those who have written about it have questioned the 1926 verdict and assumed that Mrs Hall got away with murder. The Hall–Mills murders, in a disguised form, provided the basis for several novels and films in the 1920s and 1930s. More recently, the scholar of American literature Sarah Churchwell has suggested that Scott Fitzgerald took an interest in the case and that echoes of it can be found in the plot of *The Great Gatsby*.

Bertolt Brecht's First Play

On 29 September, *Drums in the Night (Trommeln in der Nacht)*, a play by Bertolt Brecht, was staged for the first time by Munich's Kammerspiele theatre company. Brecht had been born in 1898 in the Bavarian city of Augsburg where his father was the managing director of a paper mill. An iconoclast even when he was a schoolboy during the early years of the First World War (he was nearly expelled for writing an essay in which he ridiculed the idea of dying for one's country), he wrote his first play, *Baal*, in 1918 when he was a student at Munich University. It did not receive a production until five years later. In the meantime, *Drums in the Night*, an Expressionist drama about a soldier returning from the war, set against the backdrop of the left-wing Spartacist uprising, became Brecht's debut as a professionally performed playwright. Directed by Otto Falckenberg, a champion of avant-garde theatre, it featured the Austrian-born actor Erwin Faber, at the beginning of a career that was to last until the 1980s, as the soldier Andreas Kagler, and Max Schreck, the vampire from FW Murnau's film *Nosferatu* (see March), in a supporting role.

Drums in the Night was an immediate success and word soon reached Berlin. Herbert Ihering, one of Germany's most influential drama critics, travelled from the capital to Munich to see it and his response was ecstatic. 'Bert Brecht,' he wrote, 'has changed Germany's literary complexion overnight' and raved about 'the unparalleled creative force of his language' which 'you can feel on your tongue, in your gums, your ears, your spinal column...' With such praise lavished on his first work, Brecht immediately became a strong candidate to receive that year's Kleist Prize, the most significant literary prize in Germany. Since the judge for the prize was Herbert Ihering, it was no surprise when, in November, Brecht was announced as the winner. A second production of *Drums in the Night* was staged at the prestigious Deutsches Theater in Berlin the following month. The twenty-four-year-old Brecht was firmly launched on the career which was to make him one of the most admired and influential playwrights of the twentieth century.

Dick, Kerr Ladies Tour America

On 24 September an English football club played the first match of its North American tour against Paterson FC of New Jersey. There was nothing particularly unusual about that. Teams from Britain had crossed the Atlantic before in attempts to stimulate greater interest in the game in the USA. What was unusual was that the 11 which took the field against the men from Paterson were all women. The Dick, Kerr Ladies Football Club had arrived in America. The team had been established in Preston during the First World War when women workers from Dick, Kerr and Co, a tramcar manufacturer turned munitions factory, had decided to challenge the male apprentices to an informal football match. They had won and had proceeded to beat other teams in a series of charity matches. The novelty of a skilful ladies' football team had attracted publicity and they had gone from strength to strength. By 1920 they were attracting large crowds to their matches. On Boxing Day of that year, a game against St Helen's Ladies had brought an astonishing 53,000 spectators to Goodison Park, Everton's home ground, to see them.

It was all too much for the men of the Football Association. In December 1921, they banned women's football matches at their members' grounds. The mealy-mouthed excuse they offered was that they wished to protect women from the physical harm that playing football might inflict on them but it was obvious the real reason was that the success of the ladies' game was threatening the FA's own revenues. Overnight, women's teams found it difficult to locate proper, well-maintained pitches on which to play. In the autumn of 1922, the Dick, Kerr Ladies came up with a solution. They would go on tour. They lost that first match against Paterson 6-3 but they acquitted themselves well – 'We were national champions and we had a hell of a job beating them,' one Paterson player recalled – and they played eight further games against American opposition. They finished with a record of three wins, three draws and three losses. One of the most exciting matches took place on 8 October in Washington DC against the men of the city's football club. Washington were leading at the 80-minute mark but Dick, Kerr scored two goals in the last 10 minutes and the final score was 4-4. The star of the visiting team was 17-year-old Lily Parr who went on to become one of the greatest players in the history of women's football. In 2002, she was the only woman to be one of the inaugural inductees into the English Football Hall of Fame at the National Football Museum where a statue of her now stands.

Leaving Washington with a football signed by President Warren Harding as a memento of their visit, the Dick, Kerr Ladies played several more matches before sailing for home on 9 November. They returned to find the FA ban still in force. (It would remain so until 1971.) Four years later they changed their name to Preston Ladies FC and continued to play charity games and other matches on smaller grounds until 1965. Despite all the obstacles put in their way, the Dick, Kerr Ladies continued to attract crowds of several thousand throughout the 1930s.

Straw Hats Off in New York

One of the more improbable riots in American history began on 13 September and outbreaks of violence continued for eight days, resulting in injuries, arrests and the large-scale destruction of men's hats. By the 1920s, there was an unwritten rule that nobody was supposed to wear a straw hat after a certain date in September. If a man was seen wearing one beyond that date, he was thought to be fair game. His hat was likely to be snatched from his head and stamped upon. The riot began when a group of youths in the Five Points, a notoriously rough area of New York, decided to go on a hat-stomping spree. Their first targets were factory workers who took the attacks on their headgear in good humour. Things only turned nasty when the gang tried to snatch the hats from dock workers. The dockers resisted and a mass brawl soon developed. Traffic on the Manhattan Bridge was brought to a halt, the police entered the fray and arrests were made.

More violence followed on the next evening. Mobs of youths, many wielding sticks and other weapons, roamed the streets in search of men still wearing straw hats. When they found them, they destroyed the hats and beat up their owners. As a headline in the *New York Times* put it, 'Gangs of Young Hoodlums with Spiked Sticks Terrorise Whole Blocks'. The streets were strewn with broken straw hats. Two officers were walking down Third Avenue when 'ten or twelve boys armed with sticks dashed out of doorways near 109th Street'. Eight of the boys were taken to the local police station but, because they were all under the age of 15, no arrests were formally made. Instead a Lieutenant Lenihan 'lectured them and sent for their parents, recommending a good spanking for their offspring'. The newspaper does not record whether or not the parents took the lieutenant's advice.

Some incidents over the next few days proved more serious. A man named Harry Gerber made the mistake of defending his straw hat when a gang of youths wanted to destroy it. He was badly beaten and ended up in Harlem Hospital. Some of the hat-vandals were themselves injured. John Sweeney, aged only 10, joined older boys in smashing hats on Seventh Avenue but ran into the road. He was hit by a car and his leg was broken.

After just over a week of sporadic disturbances the Straw

Hat Riots of 1922 came to an end. Although they were the worst of their kind, the tradition of snatching straw hats and stomping on them continued for some years. (In 1924, a man was even killed for wearing one.) By the beginning of the next decade, the practice had more or less died out, not least because the habit of wearing a straw boater was in decline. With the disappearance of the seasonal switch from straw to felt hats, the idea that New York streets might be filled with rioters roused to fury by spotting the wrong kind of headgear came to seem ludicrous.

Battling Siki

World Heavyweight Champion Jack Dempsey may have been mostly absent from the headlines during the year, but one of the more extraordinary fighters in boxing history reached the pinnacle of his career in Europe. Battling Siki (real name, Louis Mbarick Fall) was Senegalese and, after joining the French army during the First World War, had won medals for bravery, including the Croix de Guerre and the Médaille Militaire. With the war over, Siki resumed the boxing career he had begun in 1912 and, following a string of victories, he was eventually matched against Georges Carpentier, the man Dempsey defeated in 1921. On 24 September 1922, Siki and Carpentier met in a ring in Paris for the World and European Light Heavyweight Championships. During a controversial bout, Siki floored his opponent in the sixth round. Although he was unconscious at the time, Carpentier was initially awarded the fight by the referee, who claimed that the Senegalese had fouled the Frenchman, but the ringside judges thought differently. They awarded the fight to Siki. He was to lose his title only six months later to the Irishman Mike McTigue but he was determined to enjoy his moment in the sun. He hosted lavish parties in Parisian nightclubs, surrounded by attractive women; he strolled down the Champs-Élysées with a lion cub on a lead, throwing money at passing strangers. However, Siki's life, blighted by his own self-indulgence and by the racism of the time, was soon to end in tragedy. After his defeat at the hands of McTigue, he moved to the USA, clinging to the vague hope of a match against Dempsey but it was not to be. His taste for alcohol led to drunken punch-ups in speakeasies, confrontations with the law and regular sojourns in police cells. In December 1925, he was found dead, face down in a street in Hell's Kitchen, New York. He had been shot twice in the back, possibly because of unpaid debts. He was 28 years old.

October

Radio is rapidly changing from a hobby for a small
number of amateur enthusiasts into a global mass
medium. In Britain, the BBC is established. An
American pilot achieves another aviation first. The most
influential poem in twentieth-century English literature
is published for the first time in a small magazine.
Legendary music hall star Marie Lloyd dies. In Italy,
the first fascist state comes into existence when the
king, Victor Emmanuel III, appoints Mussolini as the
nation's prime minister.

The Creation of the BBC

Before the 1920s, radio was of interest almost exclusively to a group of amateur enthusiasts and hobbyists. Today we would probably call them nerds. As the new decade dawned, however, there were increasing signs of its potential. And 1922 proved to be the year in which radio took great strides towards becoming a national and international mass medium. It was less than ten years since the new sense of the word 'broadcasting' had been invented, reportedly by an American named Charles Herrold. From his self-built station in San Jose, California, Herrold put out a programme of chat and records. He also laid claim to creating commercial radio when he accepted advertising from a local gramophone shop in return for a selection of records to play. In America, a small number of stations had followed Herrold's example and had been broadcasting news, entertainment programmes and sports reports but there was a rapid escalation in their numbers in 1922. On 9 January, KQV-AM was launched in Pittsburgh, one of the very first AM stations in the USA. Over the following months, more and more stations went on air. By the end of the year, there were in excess of 500 in the country, all catering for the needs of the rapidly growing radio audience. Not everybody was delighted. As with any new medium, there were curmudgeonly critics eager to decry what was on offer. One wrote disparagingly of 'the indiscriminate competitive jumble of phonograph music, uninteresting lectures, and disguised advertising talks which have... made up many programmes.' Most listeners seemed much happier and their numbers grew.

In February, Warren Harding had the first radio installed in the White House and, throughout the nation, millions followed the presidential example. A few months later, Harding became the first US president whose voice was heard on the radio when he dedicated a memorial to Francis Scott Key, the man who had written the lyrics to 'The Star-Spangled Banner'. Other firsts followed. In Michigan at the end of May, the Detroit News Orchestra became the world's first radio orchestra, broadcasting on the station WWJ. The 1921 baseball World Series had been the first to be broadcast, by a new station operating out of Newark, New Jersey, but October 1922 saw a determined effort to have the matches in that year's World Series aired to a much larger audience. A famous sportswriter of the day, Grantland Rice, was hired to provide commentary on the action, although he found it difficult to adjust to the new medium. Fearing that his voice was growing hoarse, he decided to take extended breaks to rest it. Silence, of course, descended during Rice's 'rest' periods and listeners were left to puzzle out what was actually happening on the field.

In Britain, the British Broadcasting Company – it didn't become a Corporation until 1927 – was officially founded on 18 October. It had emerged from a hectic period of pioneering transmissions in the early 1920s. As the new decade dawned, the Marconi Company had started to broadcast brief, half-hour-long programmes of news and gramophone records twice a day. On occasion, the more musical of their employees made their own contributions to the entertainment. When these received positive feedback, Marconi's ambitions grew. The company invited the legendary Australian opera diva, Dame Nellie Melba, to broadcast a live recital. After first proclaiming grandly that her voice was 'not a matter for experimentation by young wireless amateurs and their magic play boxes', she was persuaded to take part. When she arrived at the Marconi works, it soon became clear that Dame Nellie had little notion of how radio worked. She was taken on a tour by a proud employee who pointed out the 140-foot tall transmitters, from the top of which her voice would be broadcast to listeners around the world. 'Young man,' she boomed in reply, 'if you think I'm going to climb up there, you are very much mistaken.'

In February 1922, a radio station named 2MT began to broadcast entertainment programmes once a week from a former army hut in the Essex village of Writtle. The first transmissions were not a huge success. The signal was weak and there were complaints from the small number of listeners that the sound was muffled. After the discovery of faulty components in the transmitter and their replacement, quality soon improved. Using an announcement ('This is Two Emma Toc, Writtle testing, Writtle testing') which rapidly became familiar to the increasing number of listeners, the Marconi engineer Peter Eckersley, a cousin of the novelist Aldous Huxley, became the country's first well-known radio presenter. Eckersley had not originally intended to go in front of the microphone himself but one night, after a glass or two of good wine, he decided he would. He overran the allotted time, failed to play all the scheduled records and decided, at one point, he would sing himself. In later sessions, he performed comedy sketches on the spur of the moment and embarked on parodies of operatic arias. Listeners loved his style and he became 2MT's regular host. The station's musical output for the first few months consisted mostly of records but the company wanted a big-name star to perform live. The Danish Wagnerian tenor Lauritz Melchior seemed to fit the bill and he was willing to perform. Unfortunately, Melchior was used to projecting his voice to fill an opera house. He stepped up to the microphone and began to sing. Very powerfully indeed. It was all too much for the transmitter which went into meltdown and put the station off the air. It was only when the tenor was placed a good 12 feet away from the microphone that something approaching normal service could be resumed. For some time to come radio engineers referred to the 'Melchior Breakdown' when describing problems with damaged equipment.

Peter Eckersley went on to become the founding Chief Engineer of the BBC, although, in 1929, he was to fall foul of his puritanical boss, John Reith, after engaging in an adulterous affair with the wife of the conductor Edward Clark. (His lover, and later wife, Dorothy emerged as a Nazi sympathiser in the 1930s, worked for German broadcasters during the war and was tried in 1945 for providing support for the enemy. She served a year in prison. Eckersley himself, who was an admirer of Oswald Mosley, has been described as 'at best a foolish Fascist fellow traveller and at worst a traitor'.)

Another Marconi station, 2LO, with its transmitter located in the Strand, followed in May 1922. Like 2MT, it looked to make a mark with a high-profile broadcast but, instead of opera, it turned to boxing. Its inaugural transmission included commentary, relayed by telephone from ringside, on the bout for the World Light Heavyweight title between England's Ted 'Kid' Lewis and the French fighter Georges Carpentier. Unfortunately for English boxing fans and for the radio station, Carpentier won the fight with a KO in the first minute of the first round. The people at 2LO had to scramble to find an alternative means of filling the airtime. Despite this setback, the new medium continued to flourish. In government, a decision was made to create a single body that would be responsible for broadcasting in Britain. The BBC was born.

The first BBC news bulletins were transmitted on 14 November at 6 pm and 9 pm, read by its original 'Director of Programmes', Arthur Burrows. They included information about a speech by the Prime Minister, Andrew Bonar Law, a train robbery, fog in London, the sale of a First Folio Shakespeare and, oddly, the latest scores from a major billiards match. As an experiment Burrows read out the bulletins twice, the second time more slowly than the first, and invited listeners to let him know which they preferred. The choice of 6 pm as the time for the earliest news report was dictated by the newspaper owners who pressured the authorities into insisting that BBC news should not threaten morning sales of their papers. In the months that followed, other formats which were to become staples of BBC programming made their appearance. The first BBC 'talk' was transmitted just before Christmas, although its subject matter is unknown. The second, which went out early in 1923, was intriguingly entitled 'How to Catch a Tiger'. The first drama written specifically for radio was broadcast by the BBC. Entitled *The Truth About Father*

Christmas, it was aired on Christmas Eve 1922. (Father Christmas was played by Arthur Burrows, the same man who had read out the first news bulletin just over a month earlier.)

As programming developed, so the number of BBC stations increased in number. Transmissions from Manchester and Birmingham had begun earlier in the year. In December, broadcasting from Newcastle was launched. Despite an opening night glitch, when the sounds of a lonely dog, howling in the night at kennels near the studio, could be heard in the background of the broadcast, it was soon a success.

Ten days before Christmas 1922, the BBC made the most momentous appointment of its early history. John Reith, the devoutly religious son of a minister in the Free Church of Scotland, accepted the post of general manager. He later confessed that he had no real idea what the job would entail and wasn't even sure what was meant by the word 'broadcasting'. However, he had great faith in both himself and in God's plans for him. 'I am trying to keep in close touch with Christ in all I do,' he wrote in his diary, 'and I pray he may keep close to me. I have a great work to do.'

Reith was born in Stonehaven on Scotland's northeast coast in 1889 but the family moved to Glasgow when he was a small child and he gained his education in that city. During his engineering apprenticeship with a locomotive company he had specialised in radio communication but his career had been interrupted by the outbreak of the First World War. He joined the Fifth Scottish Rifles, later transferring to the Royal Engineers, and was badly wounded by a sniper, taking a bullet in the cheek which left a noticeable scar he carried for the rest of his life. After two years in the USA, supervising armament contracts for the Ministry of Munitions, he ended the war as a major in the Royal Marine Engineers. Returned to civilian life, he worked as the manager of a Glasgow engineering firm before applying for the job which was to make his name. Reith was to shape the BBC for the first 16 years of its existence and his residual influence can be felt a century after he was appointed. It was Reith who asserted that the BBC's purpose was to 'educate, entertain and inform' and these words still form part of its mission statement.

Bailing Out for the First Time

1922 saw a swathe of aviation firsts (see also March and September). On 20 October, Harold R Harris became the first man to save himself by bailing out of a plane with a parachute. (Parachutes had been used many times in test jumps but this was its debut in a genuine life-and-death situation.) A test pilot for the US Army Air Service at McCook Field near Dayton, Ohio, Harris was flying at a height of several thousand feet when he lost control of his plane and faced a certain crash landing. He had no option but to test out his parachute. At an altitude of about 2,500 feet he summoned up his courage and jumped from his cockpit. After free-falling for 2,000 feet, he pulled the ripcord on his parachute. It did not fail him and he floated the last 500 feet to earth, landing among grapevines in somebody's back garden. His only injury was bruising to his hands and legs from where he'd been fighting with his plane's joystick to regain control before realising that only the parachute could save him. His aircraft, a Loening monoplane, crashed into the side of a building in Dayton three blocks away. No one was injured. Harris was later awarded the United States Air Medal for 'performing a feat which is regarded as a meritorious achievement while participating in aerial flight'. He went on to a distinguished career in aviation, serving as a vice-president of Pan-American Airways.

The Waste Land

James Joyce's *Ulysses* (see February) was not the only work of lasting value and significance to be published during the year. 1922 was what more than one writer has called the '*annus mirabilis*' of literary modernism. In October, TS Eliot published what has come to be regarded as the century's most influential poem. Born in St Louis, Missouri, Eliot had studied at Harvard and the Sorbonne in Paris. After three years back in America, he had moved permanently to Europe in 1914, winning a scholarship to Merton College, Oxford. By 1922, he had spent a period working as a teacher (one of his pupils was the future Poet Laureate John Betjeman), published two volumes of his poetry (*Prufrock and Other Observations* and *Poems*) and taken up a position with Lloyd's Bank.

For much of the year, Eliot not only carried out his duties at the bank but also struggled to fulfil his dream of creating a literary magazine that would be a reflection of his own tastes and of the wide-ranging energies of European modernism. The first issue of *The Criterion*, in a print run of 600 copies, appeared in October. It was to continue to appear until the eve of the Second World War. Not everybody in the literary world would appreciate it. In 1935, George Orwell wrote in a letter to a friend that 'for pure snootiness it beats anything I have ever seen'. However, during its existence, it published writers as different as Virginia Woolf and WH Auden, WB Yeats and Marcel Proust. It became the leading literary journal of its era. The first issue included, among other pieces, a survey of contemporary German poetry by Hermann Hesse and an appreciation of *Ulysses* by the French critic Valery Larbaud.

However, the most significant contribution came from Eliot himself. Between pages 50 and 64 was the first published version of his poem *The Waste Land*. (It was to appear first in book form in the USA in December, complete with the notes which Eliot had omitted from *The Criterion*. British lovers of modernist poetry had to wait until the following year for a UK edition, published by The Hogarth Press, the publishing house established by Virginia Woolf and her husband, Leonard.) This was a work of extraordinary originality, born out of both the difficulties of Eliot's own circumstances at the time and his despair at what he saw as the disintegration of western culture in the aftermath of the First World War. As Kevin Jackson has written in his book *Constellation of Genius*, 'It would be hard to exaggerate the misery of Eliot's personal life in the years which led up to *The Waste Land*.' The poet had married Vivienne Haigh-Wood in 1915 but their relationship had rapidly become a torment to both of them. She had recurring health problems, both mental and physical, and for long periods, he was obliged to act as, in effect, her full-time carer. At other times, she had to retire to rest homes to recover. In her brief spells of well-being she was almost certainly unfaithful. There is a strong likelihood that she embarked on a brief affair with the philosopher Bertrand Russell soon after her marriage. For his part, Eliot himself could be a cold and emotionally distant husband, unsympathetic to Vivienne's needs. In later life, he confessed that, 'I came to persuade myself that I was in love with Vivienne simply because I wanted to burn my boats and commit to staying in England... To her, the marriage brought no happiness. To me, it brought the state of mind out of which came *The Waste Land*.' At the same time, the poet was utterly disillusioned with the society he saw around him. The fragmented format of *The Waste Land* mirrors his belief that a culture which had once been whole and healthy was now breaking up into constituent parts which could no longer be united or reconciled.

Eliot's earlier verse had often been met with either bafflement or irritation. One critic, Evelyn Waugh's father, Arthur, had dismissed it as 'the ravings of drunken helot'. Many of the first reviewers of *The Waste Land* were equally enraged. 'A pompous parade of erudition,' one called it. Another suggested that 'this unhappy composition should have been left to sink itself'. John Squire, editor of *The London Mercury*, a well-known literary magazine between the wars, simply threw up his hands and admitted defeat. 'I read Mr Eliot's poem several times when it first appeared,' he wrote the following year. 'I have now read it several times more. I am still unable to make head or tail of it.' However, there were also plenty who saw immediately that this was a great poem. An anonymous reviewer in the *Times Literary Supplement* wrote that there was 'no other modern poet who can more adequately and movingly reveal to us the inextricable tangle of the sordid and the beautiful that make up life.' The American poet Conrad Aiken hailed it as 'unquestionably important, unquestionably brilliant.'

Despite both the acclaim and the denigration, probably only a relatively small number of readers would have been aware of Eliot's groundbreaking poem. More would have heard of a new collection, *Late Lyrics and Earlier with Many Other Verses*, by the grand old man of English literature at the time, Thomas Hardy. And for many poetry lovers the great event of October 1922 was a book published only a few days after the inaugural issue of *The Criterion*. AE Housman's *A Shropshire Lad* had appeared in 1896 and been a huge success. Since then, admirers of the Cambridge don's melancholy, romantic poetry had been awaiting a second volume of his verse. This finally arrived in the form of *Last Poems*. 'Not all the old gods of literature,' as Kevin Jackson has noted, 'were dead.' Housman's book rapidly became a bestseller.

Death of Marie Lloyd

In 1922, music halls constituted one of the most popular forms of mass entertainment and the biggest venues could attract large audiences each night. Veteran performers, who had made their names in the Victorian era, like Albert Chevalier ('Knocked 'Em in the Old Kent Road') and the so-called 'Prime Minister of Mirth', George Robey, were still performing. New acts like Max Miller were coming to the fore. Sadly, 7 October saw the death of Marie Lloyd, perhaps music-hall's greatest ever star. She had been loved by both working-class audiences and intellectuals, including TS Eliot who wrote an essay in praise of her after her death. In an obituary the *Manchester Guardian* praised her as 'an artist with a touch of genius', although it was obliged to admit that 'she gave pretty gross offence, at times, to delicate ears'.

Born Matilda Wood in 1870, she called herself Bella Delmere when she first appeared onstage as a teenager but she soon changed her name to the one by which she is remembered. Under this new identity she became a big star and, with songs such as 'Don't Dilly Dally', 'The Boy I Love Sits Up in the Gallery' and 'One of the Ruins That Cromwell Knocked About a Bit', she gained a popularity she never lost. Her songs ranged from the sentimental to the risqué but were all expressive of a particularly Cockney resilience in the face of life's difficulties. She needed that resilience offstage because her life had more than its fair share of problems. She was married three times to husbands who proved more trouble than they were worth and she had, by the time of her death, become increasingly dependent on drink.

Her last years were blighted by ill health but she continued to perform and was still much loved by her fans. The beginning of October saw her at crisis point, although she refused to go quietly into the night. Defying her doctors, she appeared at the Empire Music Hall in Edmonton but was unsteady on her feet and, at one point, fell over. Many members of the audience assumed the tottering about the stage was all part of the act and roared with laughter. Her final appearance was at the Alhambra Theatre, which was on the site of what is now the Odeon, Leicester Square. She was taken ill there and returned home where she died of heart and kidney failure three days later. Vast crowds, estimated at close to 50,000, attended her burial in Hampstead Cemetery.

Fascists March on Rome

In Italy, 1922 was marked by growing political instability, by clashes throughout the country between right and left and by the rise to power of the Fascist leader Benito Mussolini. Mussolini had been born in Predappio, a small town in the Emilia-Romagna region, in 1883. The son of a socialist blacksmith and a devoutly Catholic schoolteacher, he proved an intelligent, if troublesome, pupil at the various schools to which he was sent. His early life included a period in self-imposed exile in Switzerland, where he fled to avoid compulsory military service, time teaching and a number of years working as a journalist for assorted left-wing newspapers. He even wrote a novel, *Claudia Particella, L'amante del Cardinale*. A kind of historical bodice-ripper about the sex life of a seventeenth-century cardinal, it was published in serial form in the socialist newspaper of which Mussolini was then assistant editor. (After *Il Duce* came to power, his youthful literary folly was unearthed and republished. It was even translated into English under the title of *The Cardinal's Mistress*.) During the First World War, he was an advocate of his country's intervention in the conflict and was expelled from the Italian Socialist Party. After service in the war (he was wounded in action in 1917), Mussolini returned to politics and journalism but he had now lost all faith in socialism. Instead, in 1921, he created his own party, the Partito Nazionale Fascista (PNF), which rapidly gathered supporters.

The following year saw a number of violent demonstrations of the growing power of the Fascisti. May proved a particularly troubled month. In several cities, Mussolini's supporters rioted in response to the general strike called for by left-wing parties. In June, as many as 15,000 of them rampaged through the streets of Bologna, known as a stronghold of Italian socialism, torching public buildings and beating up anyone they encountered. Mussolini and the PNF now had growing national, indeed international, recognition. Later that same month an American journalist working for the *Toronto Daily Star* was granted an audience with Mussolini. The journalist's name was Ernest Hemingway and he was pleasantly surprised by the man he met. 'He is not the monster he has been pictured,' he reported. However, Hemingway had few illusions about the Blackshirts. In another article written for a Toronto newspaper that month, he wrote, 'They had a taste for killing under police protection and liked it.'

Meanwhile, the official Italian government was in turmoil. The Prime Minister, Luigi Facta, resigned on 19 July but, in the absence of any viable alternative, he returned only a fortnight later. By this time, the country was edging uncomfortably close to civil war. On 6 October, Mussolini declared to a large gathering in Milan that, 'In Italy, two governments exist – a fictitious one, run by Facta, and a real one, run by Fascists. The first of these must give way to the second.' Eighteen days later, at the Fascist Congress in Naples, he upped the rhetoric even further. 'Either the government will be given to us,' he thundered in a rabble-rousing speech, 'or we will seize it by marching on Rome.' His assembled supporters responded with roars of 'Roma! Roma!'

Despite its resounding name, the March on Rome was not as impressive a demonstration of Fascist power as was later claimed. In truth, it consisted of some 20 to 30,000 ill-disciplined Blackshirts who converged on the capital from several directions. Mussolini himself only joined it briefly, posing for photo opportunities in the midst of admiring supporters. Most members of the Fascist militia halted about 20 miles outside Rome and, during a heavy downpour of rain, many decided they had had enough and headed off home. Any rebellion could have been easily thwarted if the political will to do so had been there but it was not. Facta, still prime minister, wanted to declare martial law and use the army against the Blackshirts but any such declaration needed the king's signature. King Victor Emmanuel III, fearing civil war, refused to sign.

On 29 October, the king appointed Mussolini as Prime Minister. Victor Emmanuel thus avoided the military confrontation which the March on Rome threatened but he handed the reins of government to the National Fascist Party. 'In Italy the Fascists have attained power through a *coup d'état*,' the Anglo-German writer, diplomat and politician, Count Harry Kessler, wrote in his diary. 'If they retain it, then this is an historic event which can have unforeseeable consequences, not only for Italy but the whole of Europe.' Kessler, of course, was right. Mussolini arrived in Rome on 30 October. He had travelled by train rather than marching with his followers and he began immediately to consolidate his power. His Blackshirts flooded into the city and their march through its streets turned into a victory parade. One of his lieutenants, Giuseppe Bottai, unleashed squads of Fascisti on the working-class district of San Lorenzo, known as a hotbed of socialism, and, in the ensuing violence, 13 people were killed and hundreds injured.

Resistance to Mussolini's takeover continued. Turin was a centre for socialist and trade union activity but, in December, it became the setting for a particularly ruthless and bloody assault by Fascists on their opponents. Union buildings were burned to the ground; the printing presses of left-wing newspapers were destroyed and their editors threatened; and at least a dozen communists and socialists were killed. Pietro Ferrero, an anarchist and trade union leader, was tortured and dragged through the city streets, tied to the back of a truck.

And, in Munich, a Nazi Party official named Hermann Esser, addressing a meeting in the city's Hofbrauhaus, confidently announced that, 'Germany's Mussolini is called Adolf Hitler.' Hitler himself had not had an entirely successful year. He had spent a month of it in jail. In September 1921, he and several other members of his National Socialist Party (including Hermann Esser) had caused a ruction in a Munich *Bierkeller* where a political rival named Otto Ballerstedt was holding a meeting. They had stormed the stage from which Ballerstedt was speaking, attacked him and dragged him from the *Keller*. In January 1922, Hitler and his fellow Nazis were put on trial. He and Esser were convicted and sentenced to 100 days in prison. In the event, Hitler served only a month of his sentence, spending the days between 24 June and 27 July in Stadelheim Prison, Munich.

1922 was, however, the year in which word of this right-wing agitator began to spread outside Germany. In November, the *New York Times* published its first article about Hitler, acknowledging his oratorical powers and the 'uncanny control' he exercised over his audiences in Bavaria. The *Times* journalist also became the first of many in the English-speaking countries to underestimate Hitler and misunderstand the anti-Semitic beliefs he was loudly propagating. His anti-Semitism, the reporter said, was 'not so genuine or violent as it sounded' and that he was merely using it 'as a bait to catch masses of followers'. The years to come would show just how wrong the *Times* writer was.

November

The author of a spy novel is executed in Dublin and other Irishmen face firing squads as the civil war pits old allies against one another. Across the Atlantic, the Ku Klux Klan chooses a Texas dentist as its new leader. In a British general election, the Tories come to power after the fall of Lloyd George's coalition government and the Labour Party doubles its numbers of seats in the House of Commons. Within less than two years it will form a government for the first time. In London, the Metropolitan Police Commissioner very nearly becomes the victim of a bizarre murder plot. After more than six centuries, the Ottoman Empire ceases to exist and its last sultan is taken into exile. Albert Einstein wins the Nobel Prize for Physics. In Egypt, Howard Carter makes the archaeological discovery of the century. In Paris, the novelist Marcel Proust dies, his last word reported to be 'Mother!' The first female senator in US history spends one day in office.

The Execution of Erskine Childers

On 24 November, Erskine Childers was executed by firing squad at Dublin's Beggars Bush Barracks. Born in London, he came, on his mother's side, from an Anglo-Irish landowning family and was an ardent supporter of the Irish nationalist cause for much of his adult life. To the general public in Britain, he was probably best known as the author of *The Riddle of the Sands*, first published in 1903 and often described as the first spy novel, but he had smuggled guns to the republicans in Ireland just before the outbreak of the First World War and had served as secretary-general to the Irish delegation which had negotiated the Treaty of December 1921. Like de Valera and others, he had become resolutely opposed to some of the provisions of the Treaty, particularly the requirement of Irish leaders to swear allegiance to the British monarch. In the Irish Civil War, he had no hesitation in joining the anti-Treaty side, thus making himself a target for the pro-Treaty government. Under emergency resolutions passed in the Dáil in September, the carrying of unlicensed firearms had become a capital offence and it was for this that Childers was arrested on 10 November. He was swiftly tried before a military court and found guilty.

In his cell before his execution, Childers wrote to his wife, 'I believe God means this for the best for us, Ireland and humanity... Dead I shall have a better chance of being understood and of helping the cause – I am, as I sit here, the happiest of men.' He faced death with courage and sangfroid. 'Take a step or two forwards, lads,' he is reported to have said to the members of his firing squad, 'it will be easier that way.' Other executions of anti-Treaty leaders in the ongoing civil war followed. Rory O'Connor, the man who had led the occupation of the Four Courts earlier in the year, was shot on 8 December, together with three other republicans who had been captured when the buildings had been retaken. In an indication of the terrible divisions the civil war had engendered, the order for his death was signed by Kevin O'Higgins. O'Connor had been best man at O'Higgins's wedding the previous year. Just over 50 years later, Erskine Childers's son, Erskine Hamilton Childers, became the fourth President of Ireland.

A New Leader for the Ku Klux Klan

This was an era in which the white supremacist group, the Ku Klux Klan, was enjoying a revival. The original Klan had been established in the immediate aftermath of the American Civil War but its influence had faded by the 1870s. In 1915, the release of DW Griffith's epic film *The Birth of a Nation*, which glorified the actions of the first Klan, renewed interest in it and a second Klan was founded that same year by a preacher named William Simmons. Together with a group of friends, Simmons climbed Stone Mountain, Georgia in near freezing temperatures, burned a cross at its summit and declared himself to be Imperial Wizard of the Invisible Empire of the Knights of the Ku Klux Klan. By 1922, the second Klan had grown in numbers and it was aiming to infiltrate all corners of white American life. Special Klan weddings, baptisms and funerals took place. There were Klan picnics and days out. Offshoot organisations like the Junior Klan and the LOTIE (Ladies of the Invisible Eye) sprang up. The latter was a group which zealously policed the morals of other women. In one widely publicised event, members of the LOTIE in Fort Worth, Texas administered a 100-lash flogging to a mother whom they had decided was a bad influence on her daughter.

However, Simmons's leadership of the KKK was under challenge. In November, at the Thanksgiving Klonvocation – the Klan enjoyed making up ever more absurd words which included the letter 'K' – he was ousted by a dentist from Dallas named Hiram Wesley Evans who took over as Imperial Wizard. Under Evans's control, the organisation continued to expand. Unlike its first incarnation which had drawn support almost exclusively from the defeated South, the second Klan had members throughout the Southern states, the Midwest and the West.

The second Klan was anti-Catholic and anti-Semitic and, as the Inglewood Raid (see August) showed, it had an animus against bootleggers, but, like the first Klan, its principal targets remained African Americans. Lynchings were still horribly regular events. Data compiled by the Tuskegee Institute in Alabama shows that numbers fell dramatically in the course of the decade, from 61 in 1920 to 10 in 1929 but our year of 1922 witnessed more than 50. An anti-lynching bill was introduced into Congress by a Republican politician named Leonidas C Dyer. It passed the House of Representatives in January 1922 by a wide margin but was defeated in the Senate at the end of the year when Democrat senators from the South refused to accept it. Two further attempts to pass it later in the decade also failed. Black deaths at the hands of white mobs continued.

The Death of Liberal England

On 19 October a meeting of Tory MPs was called at the Carlton Club to discuss the pros and cons of the coalition with Lloyd George's Liberals. Party leader Austen Chamberlain and other senior figures were in favour of continuing the arrangement but they proved to be in a minority. Led by Andrew Bonar Law and Stanley Baldwin, rank-and-file MPs rebelled. In an impassioned speech, Baldwin said of Lloyd George, 'He was described to me... as a dynamic force. I accept those words. He is a dynamic force and it is from that very fact that our troubles... arise. A dynamic force is a terrible thing. It may crush you but it is not necessarily right.' More backbench Tories agreed with Baldwin than did with Chamberlain. They voted against the coalition by 187 to 87.

It is often wrongly assumed that the Tory 1922 Committee of backbench MPs, still in existence today, had its origins in this meeting. In reality, and confusingly, the 1922 Committee was formed in 1923. However, other consequences of the Carlton Club meeting were immediate and dramatic. Without Tory support, Lloyd George could not hope to command the confidence of the Commons. He resigned three hours after the vote. Chamberlain decided he could no longer remain as Tory leader and he was replaced by Bonar Law who was invited to form a government. A general election was now inevitable.

It took place on Wednesday 15 November. The Conservatives ended with the most seats (344), although this was actually 35 fewer than they had won in the previous election. It was nonetheless enough to give them a working majority. The Liberals were fundamentally and decisively split. Lloyd George presided over the National Liberals who lost 74 seats; another former prime minister, Herbert Asquith, commanded the loyalty of 62 MPs in the new parliament. Perhaps the biggest winner in this 1922 election was the Labour Party, under JR Clynes, who took 142 seats, more than doubling its representation in the House of Commons. Despite this success, Clynes was almost immediately replaced as leader by Ramsay MacDonald. This was also the first election in which the Communist Party of Great Britain put forward candidates. Shapurji Saklatvala, one of two Communists officially endorsed by the Labour Party, was also notable as the fourth ethnic Indian to serve as a British MP. Much the greatest impact of the 1922 election, however, was upon the Liberal Party which had been one of the two great forces in British politics for decades. In effect, the voting in November saw the end of an era and the Liberals never regained the position they had lost.

A Strange Case of Poisoning

On 9 November, the Metropolitan Police Commissioner, Sir William Horwood, received a box in the post. Opening it, he found it contained Walnut Whip chocolates. Thinking they were a gift from his daughter Beryl, he popped one in his mouth. Within minutes he was in agony. 'My God! Perhaps I have been doped,' he is reported to have told his secretary who was insisting that one of the walnuts must have been off. After inspecting the package in which the chocolates had arrived, and still in great pain, he summoned medical help. In fact, he'd been poisoned with arsenic contained in weedkiller which had been injected into the chocolates. Only his self-restraint in eating but a single walnut whip and the swift attention of doctors saved his life. An investigation revealed that the man who had sent the poisoned chocolates was a gentleman from Balham named Walter Tatam. Tatam had also sent a selection of poisoned chocolate eclairs to other senior police officers but none of these men had eaten any of them. His motives in trying to kill Horwood and his fellow policemen were never adequately explained. He claimed in court that he had been regularly hearing voices addressing him from suburban garden hedges and was judged to be insane.

End of Empire

As new nations emerged to claim a place on the world map, an old empire was dying. The Ottoman Empire had been in existence for more than six centuries. At its peak in the sixteenth century under Suleiman the Magnificent, it had been one of the largest empires in history and ruled territories from Bulgaria to North Africa, from Hungary to Syria. For much of the nineteenth century, it had been the

'Sick Man of Europe' as its Balkan territories increasingly agitated for independence and its slow decline triggered rivalries and disputes between other great powers. In the last decades of that century and the early years of the twentieth century, it lost nearly all of its lands west of Constantinople as nations like Bulgaria and Serbia fought for and won their independence. The First World War, and the shrinking empire's alliance with Germany, proved a disaster.

Its last sultan, Mehmed VI, was already in his mid-fifties when he came to the throne in July 1918. He had barely succeeded his half-brother as sultan when his empire had to face the consequences of defeat. The victorious allies began to divide up his lands. Mehmed VI clung on to the paltry remnants of imperial power but new forces were, literally, on the march in Turkey. An alternative centre of power, the Turkish Grand National Assembly, was established under the leadership of the army general Mustafa Kemal (later to be known as Kemal Atatürk). On 1 November 1922 this National Assembly abolished the Sultanate and ordered Mehmed out of Constantinople. The sultan, convinced his life was in danger, asked the British to help him leave the city. On 17 November, he and his immediate entourage were smuggled out of the imperial palace in two army ambulances. They were taken to HMS *Malaya* which was moored at the waterfront. The ship sailed for Malta with the sultan on board. On embarking, Mehmed initially claimed he was not abdicating. According to newspaper reports at the time, he emphasised that he 'was merely removing himself from immediate danger'. He would be back. However, it soon became clear that he would not. A dynasty which had ruled an empire for nearly 500 years had lost its power. Mehmed settled eventually in San Remo, his exile eased by the presence of three of his wives. He died there in 1926.

Einstein's Nobel Prize

On 10 November it was announced that Albert Einstein had won the Nobel Prize for Physics. It was also announced in November that Niels Bohr had won the Nobel Prize for Physics. The explanation for these two apparently contradictory facts is simple enough. Bohr had been awarded the 1922 Physics Prize. Einstein's award was the 1921 Prize which had been delayed. The Nobel Committee, responsible for choosing the Prize winners, had decided in 1921 that none of the nominees that year deserved it so they had, as the statutes allowed, held it over until 1922. So two great names in the history of physics were honoured in the same year. Curiously, Einstein was given his award not for his Theory of General Relativity but for 'his services to theoretical physics, and especially for his discovery of the law of the photoelectric effect'. Some have seen a subtle snub in the citation. Why recognise his comparatively obscure work on the photoelectric effect from 1905 and not his revolutionary theory of relativity? In 1922, Einstein was already by far the most famous scientist in the world but he was not universally popular. As a Jew, he was the target of anti-Semitism; as a pacifist, he had attracted the hatred of German nationalists. (In 1933, when Hitler came to power, Einstein was to renounce his German citizenship.) There were even those in his native country who dismissed his theories as, in the bizarre words of one critic, 'world-bluffing Jewish physics'.

Einstein himself knew in advance of the announcement of his Nobel Prize but, perhaps intentionally, he was not around to collect it at the award ceremony in Stockholm in December. He was on a lecture tour of Asia where he was greeted with the kind of hero-worship rarely lavished upon even the most eminent of scientists. In Japan, he was attended by huge crowds wherever he went. 'At the Chrysanthemum Festival,' one journalist reported, 'the centre of attention was neither the Empress nor the Prince Regent, everything turned on Einstein.' The scientist treated all the adulation with wry amusement. Standing on a Tokyo hotel balcony, looking down on cheering crowds, he remarked to his wife, 'No living person deserves this sort of reception. I'm afraid we're swindlers. We'll end up in prison yet.'

'Wonderful Things'

'Before the close of the year 1922,' HR Hall, a Keeper of Egyptian Antiquities in the British Museum, wrote in 1925, 'the name of the ancient Egyptian king, Tutankhamun, may have been familiarly known to a couple of hundred Egyptologists and students of Egyptology... Now his name is familiar to thousands throughout the world...' The unearthing of Tutankhamun's tomb and its treasures was the most significant archaeological discovery of the 1920s and, arguably, of the entire twentieth century. It was the result of the coming together of two very different men. Born in 1874, Howard Carter, the son of an artist and illustrator, was a professional archaeologist who had begun his own career as a teenager, copying the decorations in ancient Egyptian tombs. In his twenties, he had worked for the Egyptian Antiquities Service but had left in 1905 after a confrontation in which he had sided with local workmen in a dispute with a group of French tourists. Two years later, he began to work for the first time with Lord Carnarvon.

Eight years older than Carter, George Edward Stanhope Molyneux Herbert, 5th Earl of Carnarvon was a wealthy English aristocrat with a taste for indulging his obsessions. One of them was horse-racing; another was archaeology. Carnarvon once remarked that he would rather discover an intact ancient Egyptian tomb than own a horse that won the Derby. The first digs supervised by Carter and financed by Carnarvon were at Deir-el-Bahri, a complex of temples and tombs near Thebes. They produced interesting finds but nothing sensational. Both men hoped that they would have greater luck after Carnarvon, in 1914, gained the concession from the Egyptian government to excavate in what was known as the Valley of the Kings or the Valley of the Tombs of the Kings. The outbreak of the First World War brought an end to this work almost immediately but Carter returned to the site towards the end of 1917. By 1922, his endeavours had still not resulted in any remarkable finds. A decade earlier, another archaeologist named Theodore Davis had declared, 'The Valley of the Tombs is now exhausted.' It was beginning to look as if he had been right. A disappointed Carnarvon was about to pull the plug on the money but was persuaded to support one more season of digging. It was to prove a wise decision.

On 4 November, one of Carter's workmen stumbled on a large stone which proved to be the top of a flight of steps leading downwards. After these were dug out and cleared, part of a doorway was revealed. To Carter's surprise and delight it did not seem as if tomb robbers had ever broken through it. 'I was satisfied that I was on the verge of perhaps a magnificent find,' he wrote. He and Carnarvon had agreed to use a code when sending important telegrams to one another. On 6 November, the earl was staying at his family seat, Highclere Castle in Hampshire (recently the main location for the filming of *Downton Abbey*) when he received one of Carter's coded messages. Decoded, it read: AT LAST HAVE MADE WONDERFUL DISCOVERY IN VALLEY STOP A MAGNIFICENT TOMB WITH SEALS INTACT STOP RE-COVERED SAME FOR YOUR ARRIVAL STOP. Carnarvon's initial response was surprisingly unenthusiastic. POSSIBLY COME SOON, he wired back. After thinking about the message and Carter's obvious excitement, he decided it was time to leave Highclere and sent off a second telegram. This one simply said: PROPOSE ARRIVE ALEXANDRIA 20th. By 23 November, he was at Luxor. The tomb was uncovered once more and further excavation commenced.

In Carter's book *The Discovery of the Tomb of Tutankhamun*, the archaeologist describes the moment when he peered through the small hole he had made in the sealed door between him and the pharaoh's final resting place. As his eyes grew accustomed to the dim light, 'details of the room within emerged slowly from the mist, strange animals, statues and gold – everywhere the glint of gold.' Behind him, his colleagues were growing restless. 'I was struck dumb with amazement,' Carter continued, 'and, when Lord Carnarvon, unable to stand the suspense any longer, inquired anxiously, "Can you see anything?", it was all I could do to get out the words, "Yes, wonderful things." Disappointingly, these were probably not his actual words at the time. According to Carnarvon in a newspaper article, Carter said, less memorably, 'There are some marvellous objects here.' The archaeologist's book was ghost-written and it may well have been one of his ghost-writers, a popular novelist of the day called Percy White, who came up with the resonant phrase, 'Yes, wonderful things'.

There was, however, no doubt that Carter had made the most remarkable discoveries. 'Our sensations and astonishment are difficult to describe,' he wrote in his diary, 'as the better light revealed to us the marvellous collection of treasures: two strange ebony-black effigies of a King, gold sandalled, bearing staff and mace, loomed out from the cloak of darkness; gilded couches in strange forms... exquisitely painted, inlaid, and ornamental caskets... strange black shrines with a gilded monster snake appearing from within... a golden inlaid throne... and, lastly a confusion of overturned parts of chariots glinting with gold, peering from amongst which was a manikin.'

On 30 November the first press report of the findings appeared in *The Times* and word soon travelled around the world. Newspapers from New York to New Zealand headlined what had been unearthed in Egypt. What has been called 'Tutmania', the craze for all things Egyptian, began almost as soon as the wider public became aware of Carter's discoveries. Within a year Tutankhamun was everywhere. Bands played the 'Tutenkhamen Rag' (the spelling of the young pharaoh's name varied) and, in Paris, Cartier produced a new range of Egyptian jewellery. At the Folies Bergère cabaret in the French capital, 'Tutenkhamen's Follies' was staged with the dancing girls waving enormous ostrich-feather fans in what was imagined to be the Egyptian style. In London, the *Daily Express* announced that, 'the Tutenkhamen hat has arrived' and that it could be seen at Liberty's in Regent Street. Trademarks were sought for the pharaoh's name in everything from cigarettes and dolls to sandals and parasols. The new style in architecture and design known as Art Deco was markedly influenced by the renewed interest in Ancient Egypt. The consequences of Carter's discoveries are with us today, a century later. Tutankhamun, a ruler of only minor importance in the history of Ancient Egypt, is now the most famous of all pharaohs.

Death of Marcel Proust

On 18 November, at about 5.30 in the afternoon, Marcel Proust died. He had suffered from ill health for much of his life and, for three years, had rarely ventured outside the cork-lined room in his apartment where he worked and slept. His final illness was brought on by a cold which turned first into bronchitis and then into pneumonia. It is said that his last word was, 'Mother!' Proust's monumental work of fiction, *À la recherche du temps perdu*, often described as the finest novel of the twentieth century, had been begun in 1909. It first appeared in seven volumes, four of which were published in his lifetime (the last of these in April 1922) and three posthumously.

Proust and another great novelist, James Joyce (see February) had met for the only time earlier in the year, both guests at a supper party in a Parisian hotel. This was one of the few occasions in 1922 that the Frenchman had ventured forth into the world. The encounter had not been a resounding success. Joyce arrived late and was markedly the worse for drink. Proust arrived even later and was not at first able to talk with the author of *Ulysses*. Over the years, various claims have been made about what the two writers said to one another when they did get the opportunity to chat. Most suggest it was not a great meeting of minds. According to one version, Proust confessed, 'I have never read your works, Monsieur Joyce,' to which Joyce replied, 'I have never read your works, Monsieur Proust.' In another, Proust, who had spent much of his life hobnobbing with the upper echelons of society, reeled off a long list of aristocrats whom he suggested Joyce might know. Joyce, whose social circle was less elevated, could only respond repeatedly, 'Non, Monsieur' to each name put forward as a possible acquaintance.

Senator for a Day

On 21 November, an 87-year-old white supremacist and former slave-owner named Rebecca Latimer Felton became the first woman to be sworn in as a US Senator. She served for just 24 hours. Mrs Felton was a woman of deeply objectionable views on race. Born in Georgia in 1830, she had been married at the age of 18 and she and her husband had owned slaves in the years before the Civil War. Although she later acknowledged that 'slavery was a curse to the South', she continued to believe that white was inherently better than black and that African American men represented an ongoing threat to white female virtue. In a speech from 1898, she even advocated lynching as a means of protecting Southern belles from black male sexuality which, in her fevered imagination, was uncontrollable by any other means. 'If it needs lynching to protect woman's dearest possession from the ravening human beasts,' she told her audience, 'then I say, "Lynch" – a thousand times a week if necessary.'

How did a woman with such shocking views end up as the country's first female senator? And why did she only last a day in the role? The first thing to note is that Mrs Felton's ideas about lynching, although more trenchantly expressed than most, were not entirely out of line with those of many other Americans. Lynchings were by no means uncommon in the 1920s (see July) and the Ku Klux Klan grew in numbers and influence for much of the decade. The second is that, throughout her career, she was not primarily known for her opinions on race but as a vigorous proponent of women's rights. She rose to national prominence in the 1880s and 1890s through her involvement first with the Women's Christian Temperance Union and then with the campaign for (white) women's suffrage. The Nineteenth Amendment to the US Constitution, which stated that the right to vote could not be denied 'on account of sex' was only passed in 1920. Plenty of male politicians were eager to ingratiate themselves with newly enfranchised women voters. When one of Georgia's seats in the Senate became vacant through the death of the incumbent, the governor sought brownie points with his female electorate by making the elderly and by now famous Mrs Felton an interim appointee. A nationwide election for the senate was scheduled for November and the governor did not expect that she would actually be sworn in before the results of that. However, Walter George, the man who won that election in Georgia, also keen to butter up women voters, waited a day before his own swearing in to allow Mrs Felton, as a symbolic gesture, to become the first woman senator. On 21 November she took the oath as a US senator; on 22 November she surrendered the seat to the lawfully elected Walter George.

December

A former polar explorer wins the Nobel Peace Prize. The first president of the Second Polish Republic lasts five days in office. A race riot sets a Florida township ablaze. In Paris, the first performance of a play by Jean Cocteau showcases the talents of some of the most brilliant names in the city's arts. The most sensational and revealing murder trial of the decade in Britain begins as a suburban woman and her 21-year-old lover face a jury at the Old Bailey, charged with killing the woman's husband. As the year draws to an end, a new state comes into being with the signing of the treaty that creates the USSR.

Peace Prize for a Polar Explorer

The beginning of 1922 had seen the death of Ernest Shackleton. At the very end of the year, another polar explorer received recognition for his work in a very different field. The Norwegian Fridtjof Nansen was older than the other great figures of the heroic age. Born in 1861, he was originally a scientist who took up exploration after studies in zoology and neurobiology. Following a trans-Greenland expedition in 1888, he devised a plan to reach the North Pole by taking advantage of the natural drift of the ice. He found a ship, the *Fram*, and made meticulous preparations. Nansen's idea was that he would deliberately allow the *Fram* to be trapped by the ice and then natural forces of the ice flow would carry it across the top of the world. In theory, Nansen's idea was brilliant; in practice it didn't work. After more than a year in the ice, it became clear that the ship would not cross the pole. Together with one companion, Hjalmar Johansen, Nansen left it in an attempt to reach the pole on foot. They failed to do so but came close before admitting defeat. After a death-defying retreat southwards they met the English explorer Frederick Jackson on Franz Josef Land and were rescued.

Returning to Norway, Nansen decided that he had had enough of exploration and turned to other activities. He was a leading figure in the campaign and negotiations which led to Norway separating from Sweden in 1905 and once again emerging as an independent, sovereign state. In the aftermath of the First World War, he became the newly founded League of Nations' High Commissioner for Refugees. Much of his work was focused on Russia where the Revolution had created hundreds of thousands of stateless individuals. An appalling famine in 1921 only exacerbated the crisis. In early July 1922, Nansen, in his role at the League, convened an international conference in Geneva. Working with refugees, he had found that one of the biggest problems was that so many of them lacked any kind of official proof of their identity and nationality. To overcome this, he persuaded many major governments to accept the validity of what came to be known as 'Nansen passports' which enabled otherwise stateless persons to cross borders safely and legally. In December 1922, he was awarded the Nobel Peace Prize for, in the words of the citation, 'his leading role in the repatriation of prisoners of war, in international relief work and as the League of Nations' High Commissioner for Refugees'. The great polar explorer had become a different kind of hero.

A Short-Lived President

From the chaos of the post-war years, a new Polish state had emerged. Its most powerful figure was Józef Piłsudski and one of his closest political associates was a former professor of hydroelectric engineering named Gabriel Narutowicz. For four years Piłsudski had led the new Poland in his role as Chief of State but, as fresh elections for president loomed, he declined to run. Instead, to the surprise of many, it was Narutowicz, with the backing of Piłsudski, who was elected as the first president of the Second Polish Republic on 11 December 1922. Liberal in his views and supported by left-leaning political parties, Narutowicz was anathema to right-wing nationalists. He was immediately the target of vicious attacks, accusing him of atheism, freemasonry and a variety of other crimes. Because he was supported by Jewish political parties, anti-Semites loathed him and dubbed him 'the Jewish President'. On his way to his first appearance at the Sejm, the Polish parliament, protesters barricaded the streets leading to it and his motorcade was pelted with mud and snowballs. Someone attempted to strike Narutowicz with a stick and another man waved a pair of brass knuckles in his face.

Five days after taking office, on 16 December, the new president attended an art exhibition in Warsaw. Just after midday, as he was chatting to a British diplomat and examining one of the exhibits, he was approached by a painter named Eligiusz Niewiadomski. Niewiadomski, who had links to right-wing parties, pulled out a revolver and fired three shots at the president. Narutowicz died almost immediately. His assassin made little attempt to escape and was taken into custody. At his trial, he stated that he had originally intended to kill Piłsudski but his murder of Narutowicz was 'a step in the fight for Polishness and for the nation'. Many on the right agreed with him and, after he was executed by firing squad in January 1923, he was hailed by some as a martyr to the nationalist cause. In the following year, several hundred baby boys in Poland were given the unusual Christian name of Eligiusz.

Perry Race Riot

In the small town of Perry, in Taylor County, Florida, the body of a 26-year-old white schoolteacher named Ruby Hendry was found on 2 December in tall grass by the side of a railroad track. She had been badly beaten and her throat cut. It was, according to the local newspaper, 'one of the most atrocious crimes in the annals of Taylor County'. News of her murder spread rapidly and whites, intent on punishing the killer, gathered in Perry from all over northern Florida and even from neighbouring states like Georgia' not 'even from further afield as Georgia. Within a few days, the police had settled upon a suspect. Charles Wright was a 21-year-old African American and he may have attracted attention simply because he had a previous criminal record.

After a lengthy manhunt, Wright was tracked down in a nearby county and, together with another young black man named Albert Young, also thought to have been involved in Ruby Hendry's murder, was taken into custody. When law officers were transporting the two men back to Perry, they were confronted by a mob of several thousand who seized Wright and Young and took them off to face a kangaroo court. Wright was tortured in order to extract a confession from him. Satisfied that he was the murderer, the mob, in the words of a contemporary newspaper account, 'proceeded to strap him to a stake pine. Wood and grass were placed at his feet, and then set on fire. The body was burned to a crisp.' Some reports claim that spectators later scrabbled among his remains for souvenirs. Wright in his agony had specifically exonerated Young who was delivered back to the authorities.

Although he was back in police custody, a smaller group of white vigilantes kidnapped Young the following day and he was also lynched. The *Florida Times* reported that, 'The negro's body, riddled with bullets, was left dangling from a tree.' White desire for mob vengeance was still not satisfied. Although neither Wright nor Young was a native of Perry, the black community in the town now became a target. Many of the vigilantes went on a rampage through the black districts, burning homes, businesses and at least one church. More lives were lost.

Cocteau's Antigone

On December 20, Jean Cocteau's version, half translation and half modern adaptation, of *Antigone* by the Ancient Greek dramatist Sophocles was staged for the first time at the Théâtre de l'Atelier in Paris. In addition to Cocteau, a remarkable selection of the most talented artists in the city worked on it. The set designs were by Picasso; the costumes by Coco Chanel; and the music by Arthur Honegger. In a very short time, Picasso, taking inspiration from Greek vases, created what has been described as 'a vast blue seaside sky, white Doric columns, and huge round shields'. Cocteau had been insistent that only Chanel, now most famous for the 'little black dress', could costume the women in his play. 'I wanted Mlle Chanel,' he wrote, 'because she is our leading dressmaker and I cannot imagine Oedipus's daughters patronising a "little" dressmaker.' The Swiss composer Honegger was so fascinated by the story of Antigone that he returned to it some years later, fashioning a three-act opera from the story with a libretto by Cocteau. Playing the role of Tiresias was Antonin Artaud, future theorist of the 'Theatre of Cruelty' and one of the most influential figures in twentieth-century theatre. At the third performance of the play, the future Surrealist leader André Breton, who was in attendance and no great fan of Cocteau, took exception to one of the lines. He loudly expressed his disapproval and the rest of the audience was treated to the extra entertainment of a noisy exchange of words between Breton and his supporters on the one hand, and Cocteau who was on stage and speaking the part of the Chorus through a megaphone.

Thompson and Bywaters

In Britain, there can be little debate about what was the most sensational trial of 1922. It came at the very end of the year. In the dock were Edith Thompson and her lover Freddy Bywaters who faced charges of killing Edith's husband, Percy. Like the Hall–Mills case in America (see September), it served up murder and adultery to the newspaper-reading public but with a peculiarly British helping of sanctimony as a side-dish. It began in December and, as it proceeded, it revealed in stark detail both the story of an individual domestic tragedy and the country's standard attitudes at the time to marriage and morality. Edith Thompson (née Graydon) was a lively, intelligent young woman, born in Dalston, East London in 1893, who had married her husband Percy after a six-year engagement in 1916. Percy, who was only three years older than his wife, soon proved a man suffering from premature middle age and, by the start of the new decade, Edith was feeling trapped in a boring, stultifying marriage. The couple were living in a suburban villa at 41 Kensington Gardens, Ilford. From the outside, Edith's life must have looked enviable. She was upwardly mobile from working to lower middle class, married to an apparently loving husband and had her own career, working for a wholesale milliner in the City. But, in reality, she was desperately unhappy.

Enter Freddy Bywaters, a handsome, eighteen-year-old merchant seaman. Edith and her family had known him since he was a child but it was only now that Edith, a romantic idealist dreaming of escape from her increasingly miserable marriage, took particular notice of him. In June 1921, she and Percy, together with Freddy and Edith's younger sister Avis (who had her own romantic interest in the young man), went on holiday to the Isle of Wight. Towards the end of the vacation, Edith and Freddy spoke together and acknowledged their attraction to one another. Percy was blind to it, so much so that, when they returned to London, he invited Freddy to rent the spare room in 41 Kensington Gardens. Just over a week after he moved in, the new lodger and Percy's wife became lovers. The day on which Edith came to Freddy 'in your little room', and they enjoyed their first sexual encounter, 27 June 1921, was his nineteenth birthday.

The love affair continued for the next 15 months but, of necessity, much of it was epistolary rather than physical. Freddy had to return to his job at sea. Over a period of 60 weeks he was on leave and in England for just over 14 of them. Even when he was in the country, Edith could not always see him and the opportunities for them to make love must have been few. Percy, by now aware of some kind of relationship between his wife and his former lodger, although perhaps uncertain of its exact nature, was jealous and watchful.

Instead they poured their feelings into letters. Few of Freddy's survive. Many of Edith's do and they played a major role in convicting her at her trial. When Freddy was away, she sent him long letters, full of the vividly described details of her everyday life and ever more extravagant declarations of her love. And some of them contained the ambiguous messages that the prosecution at her trial were to claim as evidence of attempts to kill her husband. If they were, they were half-hearted and unsuccessful but they were probably only fantasies. Edith certainly said they were. In one letter she tells Freddy, 'I used the light bulb three times but the third time – he found a piece – so I've given up – until you come home.' Was she feeding her husband ground glass from a light bulb? Possibly, but it's just as likely that she was casting herself in the role of one of the characters from the melodramatic novels she enjoyed reading. In another letter she records Percy commenting on his tea tasting bitter. 'Now I think whatever else I try it in again will still taste bitter,' she wrote, 'he will recognize it and be more suspicious still...' Her defence counsel questioned her about this during the trial. 'Was this an imaginary incident then that you were recording?' he asked. 'Yes,' Edith replied.

When Freddy returned to England for the last time in late September 1922, the stage was set for a tragedy. On 3 October, the Thompsons attended a performance of a

Ben Travers farce at the Criterion Theatre in the West End. After the show, they took the train back to Ilford and began to walk from the station to their home. As they made their way along Belgrave Road, a man emerged from the darkness, wielding a knife, and attacked Percy. With Edith screaming 'Don't, oh don't,' according to one witness, her husband fell to the pavement, dying. He suffered a dozen superficial cuts but three deep wounds, one of which penetrated the carotid artery and the jugular vein and proved fatal. Percy bled out at the scene of the assault. He was 150 yards from his home. As several witnesses testified, Edith was 'hysterical'. At one point, she said in horror, 'His blood is all over me!' At another, she spoke to the doctor who arrived on the scene. 'Why didn't you come sooner and save him?' she asked. Later, after she had been escorted back to 41 Kensington Gardens, she told the policeman with her, 'They will blame me for this.'

In her first statement to police, Edith made no mention of an attack or an attacker. She and Percy, she said, were en route from the station to their house when he was taken ill. With almost comic bathos, she reported him as calling out, 'Oo-er' before falling against her. 'I put my arm out to save him, and found blood which I thought was coming from his mouth. I tried to hold him up, he staggered several yards towards Kensington Gardens, and then fell against the wall and slid down.'

However, despite Edith's silence, Freddy Bywaters soon became a suspect. He was due to sail from England once more in a matter of days on a ship called the *Morea*, moored at Tilbury Dock, but he was taken into custody when he turned up at the house belonging to the Graydons, Edith's parents. Almost unbelievably in the circumstances, he went there to fulfil a previous promise to take Avis out to the cinema. The house was, of course, being watched. At the police station, Edith saw Freddy for the first time since the murder, by chance according to the officer in charge of the case, although it seems much more likely that the encounter was engineered by the police. Unsurprisingly, it was a shock for her. She broke down, crying out, 'Why did he do it? I didn't want him to do it! Oh God, oh God, what can I do?' It was the cue for her to change her story and acknowledge that she had recognised Freddy Bywaters as the man who had attacked her husband. Hours later, Freddy confessed to the murder, although he stated clearly, 'I did not intend to kill him.' He did not, however, sound very remorseful and his contempt for Percy was obvious. 'The reason I fought with Thompson was because he never acted like a man to his wife. He always seemed several degrees lower than a snake. I loved her and I couldn't go on seeing her leading that life.'

By this time the police had decided that Edith had incited Freddy, indeed conspired with him, to kill her husband. She was as guilty as he was and both would be charged with murder. 'Why her?' asked a bewildered Freddy when he was told. His bewilderment was unsurprising. The case against him was incontrovertible. As a tactless old lag told him during his pre-trial imprisonment in Brixton, 'You ain't got no chance, old chap, you're going to get topped.' The case against Edith, on the other hand, was almost non-existent. At least, it was – until the police, searching Freddy's cabin on the *Morea*, found a stash of letters which Edith had sent him during his earlier voyages. She had asked him to destroy them. She believed he had but now they were to be used in court to condemn her.

The trial of Edith Thompson and Frederick Bywaters opened on 6 December and the nation was immediately agog. Newspaper readers at breakfast tables across the country were absorbed by the unfolding drama. Tickets for the Old Bailey, where one could actually see the participants in it, were in high demand. A black market for them sprang into existence. Unemployed men stood all night in the queue for the public gallery and then sold their seats to what the papers called 'society ladies' for as much as £5. 'It was the atmosphere of a first night,' according to one journalist. In too many ways, the individuals in the case could be made to resemble characters in a play. As the journalist Filson Young later wrote, 'The three persons concerned were duly presented in this melodramatic way. The good, patient and unoffending husband; the manly young fellow, corrupted and debauched by the experienced woman of the world; and the black-hearted sorceress, weaving her spells, casting her nets, and bringing ruin upon everybody connected with her.'

It was all monstrously unfair. The leading pathologist of the day, Bernard Spilsbury, who had testified in the cases of Dr Crippen and George Joseph Smith, the so-called 'Brides in the Bath' murderer, could find no evidence that Percy had ever been fed any poisons. Unfortunately, despite the lack of evidence, the prosecution remained convinced, in the words of a journalist at the time, 'that if Mrs Thompson did not actually commit the murder, hers was the brain that planned the affair.' Her defence case was not helped by the many excerpts from her letters which were read out in court – passionate outpourings of feelings and imagination which were delivered to the jury and the wider public in the dry, emotionless voice of policemen and court officials. Her own decision, against the advice of her legal team, to go into the witness box was a disastrous mistake. Her performance lost rather than gained the jury's sympathy.

On Monday 11 December the jury returned with its verdict after only two hours of deliberation. Both defendants were found guilty and sentenced to death. Edith, who had to be supported by female prison warders in the dock, was reduced to near-hysteria, letting out a long, disbelieving scream. Freddy called out, 'The jury is wrong. That woman is not guilty.'

In the short period between the verdict and the scheduled execution, desperate attempts were made to commute the sentences of both Edith and Freddy. Both families addressed pleas for mercy to the Home Secretary and to the king and queen. None was of any avail. The authorities were determined that both should hang. Even Freddy's last-ditch effort to save his lover proved useless. In the presence of prison warders, he said, 'I swear she is completely innocent. She never knew that I was going to meet them that night. She didn't commit the murder. I did. She never planned it. She never knew about it... I can't believe that they will hang her.'

Yet hang her they did. At 9 am on 9 January 1923, both Freddy and Edith went to their deaths, he in Pentonville Prison and she in Holloway. It remains painful to read accounts of her execution. At times during the previous weeks, she had sounded almost resigned to her fate. In a letter to a friend, she wrote, rather beautifully, that, 'We all imagine we can mould our own lives – we seldom can, they are moulded for us – just by the laws and rules and conventions of this world, and if we break any of them, we only have to look forward to a formidable and unattractive wilderness.' However, as the date for the execution drew nearer and the efforts to save her failed, she began to fall apart. The prison governor responded by authorising the giving to her of large and regular doses of morphine. By the morning of 9 January, she was drugged up to the eyeballs and barely capable of movement. Alfred Woods, the assistant executioner, interviewed decades later, reported that, 'The other officer and I carried her to the scaffold making a seat of our hands for her. All this time she appeared to be under the influence of dope, the condemned cell smelt strongly of a hospital. We carried her to the scaffold and held her up on her feet while the executioner put the rope round her neck.' Another witness, a woman doctor named Dora Walker, speaking, like Woods, more than thirty years after the event, remembered it slightly differently. Edith, she said, was doped but conscious and she managed to walk, with assistance, from the condemned cell. As she neared the scaffold, 'She hung back and grunted as an animal going to be killed. It could not be described as a human shout or scream.' Afterwards, 'The executioner was most upset and completely broken down. He came out shouting, "Oh Christ, oh Christ".'

According to her defence counsel, Edith Thompson was 'hanged for adultery' and it is difficult to disagree with him. The evidence that she knew in advance of Frederick Bywaters' intent to murder her husband is slight to non-existent and her own fantasies of doing away with him, hinted at in her letters to her lover, were almost certainly just that - fantasies. Unfortunately, the fact that she had taken a lover eight years her junior, and rejoiced in it, was indisputable. She was condemned for her supposed immorality not for the death of Percy Thompson. It was her letters which, for many at the time, were evidence of her wickedness. 'They played a great part in hanging her,' the detective who first charged her with murder wrote. To one member of the jury, penning a letter to the *Daily Telegraph* nearly thirty years later, they were still all too fresh in his memory. '"Nauseous" is hardly strong enough to describe their contents... Mrs Thompson's letters were her own condemnation.'

Reading excerpts from them today, it is hard to see quite why they roused such strong feelings but, to many people in the Britain of 1922, they were documents of immorality. A pamphlet, published by the *Daily Express* immediately after the jury's verdict, both makes this clear and reveals the extraordinary frenzy of righteousness into which elements of the media had whipped themselves. 'The death of Percy Thompson is not the worst thing in this apocalypse,' the writer claimed. The worst thing, apparently, was 'the degradation of love into a vile caricature of its own image'. Poor Edith Thompson, according to the *Daily Express*, was a symptom of 'national decay', for 'there can be no hope for a race that loses its ancient bearings in a sea of sensual anarchy'.

The Thompson and Bywaters case has continued to attract attention and controversy throughout the century since its conclusion. In the 1930s, the writer F Tennyson

Jesse published a novel, *A Pin to See the Peepshow*, which is a very thinly disguised fictional retelling of it. Another work of fiction based on the case, *Fred and Edie* by Jill Dawson, appeared in 2000. A film, *Another Life*, starring Natasha Little as Edith, Nick Moran as Percy and Ioan Gruffudd as Freddy, was released the following year. A sacrifice to an old-fashioned morality whose grip on many people was slipping in 1922, and now seems antediluvian, Edith has not been forgotten. As her latest biographer, Laura Thompson has written, 'She is under our skin still. Her story could not, cannot, be dislodged from our collective memory.'

Formation of the USSR

As the year ended, a new nation, destined to become one of the century's superpowers, came into existence. On 29 December a draft Declaration on the Creation of the Union of Soviet Socialist Republics was signed by delegates from four Soviet Republics – Russia, Ukraine, Byelorussia and Transcaucasia. The following day the declaration, together with an accompanying Treaty on the Establishment of the USSR, was approved by the First Congress of Soviets of the USSR. The treaty assigned to the newly created Union all responsibilities to conduct foreign affairs. It controlled the armed forces and could declare war or agree peace. It could decide to expand the number of its members (it eventually encompassed 15 republics) and it created the structures through which power in the new state could be exercised. A single Soviet citizenship was brought into being, a flag decided upon and the capital of the USSR was declared to be Moscow. There were to be many other changes to the USSR in the future but the state created by the treaty signed at the end of 1922 was to last for 69 years until its dissolution in 1991 under the presidency of Boris Yeltsin.

Bibliography

1922: Portrait of a Year is intended as popular rather than scholarly history and I have not weighted down the text with footnotes and academic annotations. However, the following bibliography lists books that I have consulted while writing it and offers suggestions for further reading for those interested.

Akers, Monte, *Flames After Midnight: Murder, Vengeance, and the Desolation of a Texas Community*, Austin: University of Texas Press, 1999

Allen, Frederick Lewis, *Only Yesterday: An Informal History of the Nineteen Twenties*, New York: Harper & Brothers, 1931

Ambrose, Kevin, *The Knickerbocker Snowstorm*, Charleston, SC: Arcadia Press, 2013

Amin, Shahid, *Event, Metaphor, Memory: Chauri Chaura 1922-1992*, Berkeley: University of California Press, 1995

Angle, Paul M, *Bloody Williamson: A Chapter in American Lawlessness*, New York: Alfred Knopf, 1952

Bailey, Greg, *The Herrin Massacre of 1922: Blood and Coal in the Heart of America*, Jefferson, NC: McFarland and Company, 2020

Bathgate, Gordon, *Radio Broadcasting: A History of the*

Airwaves, Barnsley: Pen & Sword Books, 2020

Cottrell, Peter, *The Irish Civil War 1922-23*, London: Osprey Publishing, 2008

Davis, Colin J, *Power at Odds: The 1922 National Railroad Shopmen's Strike*, Urbana and Chicago: University of Illinois Press, 1997

Dunscomb, Paul E, *Japan's Siberian Intervention 1918-1922*, Lanham MD: Lexington Books, 2011

Figes, Orlando, *A People's Tragedy: The Russian Revolution 1891-1924*, London: Viking, 1997

Frayling, Christopher, *The Face of Tutankhamun*, London: Faber, 1992

Friedrich, Otto, *Before the Deluge: A Portrait of Berlin in the 1920s*, New York: Harper & Row, 1972

Ginzburg, Ralph, *100 Years of Lynchings*, Baltimore: Black Classic Press, 1988 (first published 1962)

Graves, Robert & Hodge, Alan, *The Long Weekend: A Social History of Great Britain 1918-1939*, London: Hutchinson, 1985 (first published in 1941)

Hopkins, David, *Dada and Surrealism: A Very Short Introduction*, Oxford: Oxford University Press, 2004

Hopkinson, Michael, *Green Against Green: The Irish Civil War*, Dublin: Gill Books, 2004

Jackson, Kevin, *Constellation of Genius: 1922: Modernism and All That Jazz*, London: Windmill Books, 2013

Jackson, Kevin, *Nosferatu: Eine Symphonie des Grauens*, London: BFI/Macmillan, 2013

Keogh, Dermot, *Twentieth-Century Ireland*, Dublin: Gill & Macmillan, 2005 (first published 1994)

Kinnear, Michael, *The Fall of Lloyd George: The Political Crisis of 1922*, London: Macmillan, 1973

BIBLIOGRAPHY

Lownie, Andrew, *The Mountbattens: Their Lives and Loves*, London: Blink Publishing, 2019

McAuliffe, Mary, *When Paris Sizzled: The 1920s Paris of Hemingway, Chanel, Cocteau, Cole Porter, Josephine Baker and their Friends*, Lanham, MD: Rowman & Littlefield, 2016

Milton, Giles, *Paradise Lost: Smyrna 1922*, London: Sceptre, 2008

Moore, Lucy, *Anything Goes: A Biography of the Roaring Twenties*, London: Atlantic Books, 2008

Rabaté, Jean-Michel (ed.), *1922: Literature, Culture, Politics*, Cambridge: Cambridge University Press, 2015

Stashower, Daniel, *Teller of Tales: The Life of Arthur Conan Doyle*, New York: Henry Holt, 1999

Thompson, Laura, *Rex v. Edith Thompson: A Tale of Two Murders*, London: Head of Zeus, 2018

Wagg, Stephen (ed.), *Myths and Milestones in the History of Sport*, London: Palgrave Macmillan, 2011

Acknowledgements

My thanks should first of all go to Ion Mills, publisher *extraordinaire*, who had the original idea for this book. I hope, now it's finished, he's pleased with what has finally emerged from our email conversations in early 2020. I would also like to thank all of Ion's colleagues at Oldcastle Books whose friendliness and professionalism make dealing with the company such a pleasure: Claire Watts, Lisa Gooding, Ellie Lavender, Hollie McDevitt. Elsa Mathern has provided the book with a fine cover and I am grateful for the copy-editing and proofreading skills of Jayne Lewis and Madeleine Hamey-Thomas.

As always, friends and family have provided encouragement. Love and thanks to my sister, Cindy Rennison, and to my mother, Eileen Rennison. For more than a year I have been unable to see my family in Germany – Wolfgang, Lorna and Milena Lüers – save in Zoom calls but they have been much in my thoughts. As a professional historian himself, Hugh Pemberton gave me confidence that my approach to research wasn't entirely amateurish. Dr Kevin Chappell, a good friend since our college days, has a wide knowledge of twentieth-century Irish history which helped to point me in the direction of several useful books. During the weird times in which this book was written, contact with friends has been almost entirely restricted to emails and phone conversations but thanks to David Jones, John Magrath, Susan Osborne, Richard Monks, Travis Elborough, Andrew Holgate and Graham Eagland who all took an interest in the book. Neighbours Jamie and Lucy Campbell recommended that I should read Bill Bryson's *One Summer* (I only hope my book is one tenth as enjoyable) and always asked about *1922*'s progress during conversations over the garden fence.

In the writing of this book, as in all the work I do, my biggest debt is to my wife Eve whose love, support and encouragement are ever present.

Index

●LDCASTLE BOOKS

POSSIBLY THE UK'S SMALLEST
INDEPENDENT PUBLISHING GROUP

Oldcastle Books is an independent publishing company formed in 1985 dedicated to providing an eclectic range of titles with a nod to the popular culture of the day.

Imprints vary from the award winning crime fiction list, NO EXIT PRESS, to lists about the film industry, KAMERA BOOKS & CREATIVE ESSENTIALS. We have dabbled in the classics, with PULP! THE CLASSICS, taken a punt on gambling books with HIGH STAKES, provided in-depth overviews with POCKET ESSENTIALS and covered a wide range in the eponymous OLDCASTLE BOOKS list. Most recently we have welcomed two new digital first sister imprints with THE CRIME & MYSTERY CLUB and VERVE, home to great, original, page-turning fiction.

oldcastlebooks.com

| OLDCASTLE BOOKS | KAMERA BOOKS | HIGHSTAKES PUBLISHING
| POCKET ESSENTIALS | CREATIVE ESSENTIALS | THE CRIME & MYSTERY CLUB
| NO EXIT PRESS | PULP! THE CLASSICS | VERVE BOOKS